Finding Vinland

Unearthing Evidence for Viking Presence in North America

Finding Vinland

Unearthing Evidence for Viking Presence in North America

Alexandra Gross

Gina Schopfer

Taylor Croft

Austin Mardon

Catherine Mardon

Edited by Jessica Jutras

Design by Clare Dalton

First Printing: 2020

Typeset and Cover Design by Clare Dalton

Book cover font: *The Fell Types are digitally reproduced by Igino Marini. www.iginomarini.com*

ISBN 978-1-77369-197-8

Golden Meteorite Press

103 11919 82 St NW

Edmonton, AB T5B 2W3

www.goldenmeteoritepress.com

Table of Contents

Introduction: Discovering the New World

In 1492, Columbus sailed the ocean blue. Without hesitation, North Americans, both young and old, can recite this popular rhyme learned from their schooldays. It was an effective tool to help history students memorize the date that the Italian explorer, Christopher Columbus, discovered the "New World." Although Columbus tends to stick in many minds as the explorer responsible for the settlement of North America, the school curriculum also teaches Canadian students about another Italian explorer by the name of John Cabot, who arrived in Atlantic Canada in 1497 and claimed the land for England on behalf of King Henry VII. The later arrival of the French explorer, Jacques Cartier, is also taught in detail. Cartier claimed the Gaspé Peninsula for King Francis I in 1534, and from that point on, attempted repeatedly to establish French Settlements.

Though many of these first attempts failed, they marked the beginning of permanent European settlement in Canada, and many contemporary geographical place names are derived from those initial sites established in the seventeenth century. Between the years of 1663 and 1673, a large collective of French women - called Les Filles du Roi - immigrated to Canada to marry French men through a sponsorship program established by King Louis XIV. This program was meant to address the problem of male French settlers expressing a reluctance to remain in New France permanently, due to a lack of women. This initiative was ultimately successful, and these women became the founding mothers of French Canadians.

While provincial school curriculums in Canada have taught First Nations history for many years, there has been a recent shift from teaching a history that emphasizes friendly trade relations between Europeans settlers and Indigenous tribes to one that acknowledges the violence carried out against these Indigenous peoples by European settlers, not just historically, but to the present day. The old discourse of North America as empty, unpopulated land has been widely contested in recent years. Indigenous persons have been in present-day North America for at least 17,000 years, beginning when sea levels fell and early peoples crossed the Beringia land bridge from Siberia, arriving in Alaska and the Yukon. Approximately 1000 years after this initial migration, the Laurentide Ice Sheet melted and these people moved further south and east into Canada and the United States, eventually spanning the entirety of the land.

As historians acknowledge, history is extremely subjective. Winston Churchill is often credited with the phrase, *history is written by the victors*. Ironically, it is widely contested whether Churchill came up with this himself or copied the writings of others. While it is true that history is often biased according to the perspective of the person writing it, its subjectivity goes further than this. Knowledge about the past is obtained using two primary methods: through the analysis of historical records – written by other biased persons whose biases cannot be fully known – and the discovery of physical archaeological evidence. Most of what is labeled as an historical fact is essentially a well-informed guess.

The further into the past one ventures, the less certain one can be about its events. Take, for example, the events that took place during the life of Boudica, an Iceni (Celtic) queen who died almost 2000 years ago. At this time in history, the Romans had invaded Great Britain, and although they had coexisted with the Celtic tribes up until this point well enough, they were beginning to treat the native people with force and violence. Boudica raised an army against the Roman legions and won several battles against them. Most of what is known about Boudica and the uprising is derived from an account given by a Roman called Tacitus.

On the BBC podcast, *You're Dead to Me*, historian Dr. Emma Southon says that almost everything known about Boudica may not actually be true.[1] The only thing known with certainty is that she was a real person. It was popular at the time to write historical events as literature and art, and Tacitus essentially retells the classic Roman story of the Rape of Lucretia, thereby making Boudica a symbolic story about how Rome has become out of control and tyrnanical.[2]

---

1   Emma Southon, "Boudica," You're Dead to Me, hosted by Greg Jenner (BBC Radio 4, September 13, 2019), Podcast.

2   Southon, "Boudica."

Tacitus also claimed that she ended her life with poison, which was seen as a very weak, feminine death; this assertion is unlikely to be true and was probably written to discredit her.[3]

The information we claim as "fact" is massively subjective, as is the decision about which facts and stories should be emphasized and which are considered less important. In the Canadian school curriculum, one such history that is essentially ignored is the presence of another group of Europeans in North America, who arrived over 500 years before John Cabot: the Vikings.

Around the year 1000 CE, Vikings arrived on the shores of Atlantic Canada during an expedition arranged by Leif Erikson. Written evidence for their presence in North America can be found in documents written as early as the 13th century, though no archaeological evidence was found to corroborate these records until a Norse settlement was conclusively discovered in Newfoundland in 1960. In the sixty years since this discovery, their presence in Canada has largely continued to be ignored in the curriculum. It is the history of the explorations of these Vikings in North America that will be the main focus of this book.

Before going any further, a pause must be taken to define what, exactly, the term *Viking* means. It is usually used to refer to a segment of the Scandinavian population that lived between the late 8th and 11th centuries. These Norsemen went abroad with the intention of finding fortune and fame to bring back home.[4] *Scandinavians* include persons from Denmark, Norway,

---

3   Southon, "Boudica."

4   "What does the word Viking mean?" Hurstwic, n.d., http://www.

and Sweden. In this sense, being a Viking does not refer to one's ethnicity, but rather their occupation. Vikings also almost always refer to men, though some historians have argued for the existence of Viking women as well.

Another point of confusion is that Vikings are sometimes called *Norsemen*, meaning *north men*. This term applies to Vikings from all of Scandinavia, as they all spoke a common Norse language. However, the term *Norse* is also sometimes used to specifically apply to persons from Norway. In this book, when Vikings from Norway are exclusively being referred to, the term *Norweigan Vikings* will be used, and the term *Norse* will be used to refer to Vikings from all of Scandinavia. The term *nordic* can also be confusing; this refers to contemporary persons from Scandinavia, as well as Finland, Iceland, Greenland, and the Faroe Islands. This term will not be frequently used in this book; terminology will be as specific as possible.

In 750 CE, Scandinavians were presented with the problem of overpopulation and a scarcity of land fit for growing crops.[5] As knowledgeable seafarers, the most plausible solution to these problems was to venture out to new lands. Christian texts often referred to Vikings as "evildoers," likely due to both their pagan religion as well as their raiding activities, which were often perpetrated against Christian countries.[6]

While Vikings undoubtedly perpetrated violence and are known for pillaging, contemporary research questions whether

hurstwic.org/history/articles/text/word_viking.htm

5   "The Vikings in Scotland," Crann Tara, last modified 2006, https://cranntara.scot/vikings.htm.

6   What does the word Viking mean?

they were as violent as they have historically been portrayed. Some research suggests that they were no more violent than other invading groups at the time, and may have actually been less violent than some, such as the Franks.

In the 19th century, there was a renewed interest in Viking-era history.[7] This period of time in Western societies was called the *Romantic era* and rose as a reactionary response to enlightenment rationalism. This era emphasized emotion, creativity, heroics, and the learning of folk societies,[8] thus Vikings began to be viewed not as evildoers but rather as adventurers, despite the fact that some atrocities were undoubtedly committed during raids.[9]

Readers unfamiliar with Vikings are likely to conjure images of tall, blonde, and savage Norsemen with brightly painted shields and horned helmets. This image stems from Romanticist accounts and is inaccurate, thus in *Part One* of this book, popular misconceptions of Vikings will be dispelled with facts. *Part One* will also explore the cultural background of the Vikings. Although the focus of this book is the discovery of North America by the Vikings, an analysis cannot be done without understanding these explorers first as Norse people. Important cultural aspects will include Norse geographical areas of derivation, shared spoken language, religious beliefs, styles of art, and political structures.

---

7 What does the word Viking mean?

8 "Romanticism," Encyclopaedia Britannica, last modified March 27, 2020, https://www.britannica.com/art/Romanticism

9 What does the word Viking mean?

Part Two will provide an overview of the impact of Viking exploration and expansion across the world, including the British Isles, Europe, The Middle East, and North Africa. A special emphasis will also be placed on their settlement of Iceland and Greenland, as these are the countries from which the Vikings who set foot on North American soil were from.

In *Part Three*, written evidence of Viking presence in North America will be explored. The primary sources for this evidence come from the Sagas of Icelanders, specifically The Saga of Greenlanders and The Saga of Erik the Red. Although these sagas are written in heroic prose, giving them a fictional, story-like quality to them, they are largely understood to contain a high degree of historical fact. The accounts within these sagas are corroborated by other contemporary works, such as Adam Bremen's *Descriptio Insularum Aquilonis* (written between the years of 1072 and 1081), which includes a conversation he had with the Danish king in which a new land called *Vinland* is mentioned. The term *Vinland*, or wine-land, is the name given to an area of Eastern Canada, and is named so due to the area being abundant in wild grapes. Sigurd Stefansson produced a map of Vinland in 1570, and a place called Vinland appears numerous times in other Icelandic chronicles written over the centuries.

Finally, *Part Four* will analyze the physical archaeological evidence for Viking presence in North America. Readers will gain a thorough understanding of the definitive archaeological evidence that has been discovered so far, as well as gain insight into the work currently being done in this area. The most complete archaeological evidence of Viking presence is that of the site of L'Anse Aux Meadows. A site known as Hóp in written records is currently being searched for by archaeologists, and recent discoveries in this area have been made. This section will finish with a discussion of artifacts and sites that some have claimed to be Viking-made, though most are either outright hoaxes or mistaken Indigenous archaeology.

Part One:

Vikings and Norse Culture

Distinguishing Fact from Myth

Those unfamiliar with Vikings probably have an idea of the culture fueled by misconceptions perpetuated by mainstream media that greatly differ from the actual lives and practices of these people. Imagery of Vikings in everything from art to product branding to popular culture have made Vikings one of the most recognizable cultures of the historic past, however it has also seemed to add to the phenomena of the Vikings being one of the most incorrectly stereotyped cultures as well.

One of the greatest misconceptions being what it actually means to be a Viking. The term Viking, as used in phrases such as Viking civilization, the Viking age or the Viking Movement, is often used as a convenient way to broadly describe the civilization of the Scandinavian people between the 8th and 11th centuries. However, used correctly, the term refers rather to the act of the Scandinavian people leaving their homeland to venture out to raid, trade and pillage in new land. As the Scandianvias populations grew, so did the problem of scarcity of land. To go Viking offered a solution to this problem by venturing to and conquering more fertile lands as a means of accommodating the growing population. As they were already skilled seafarers, Danish, Norweigan and Swedish crews set sail aboard their characteristic longships to find more suitable farming land than the often rocky and sandy environments they came from.[10] Not all Scandinavian people went Viking, but rather to be a Viking was among the many ways an individual could choose to contribute to their civilization. Therefore, although all Vikings were Scandinavian, not all Scandinavians were Vikings, and the term refers to an occupation of this time rather than the whole of the people themselves.

A romanticized conception of the men on these expeditions likely brings forth visions of burly, blonde bearded warriors in the iconic horned helmets storming the beaches of new land. This popular image seemed to originate in the 19th century by artists of nationalities other than Scandinavian, who seemed to lack the proper knowledge of the individuals they were depicting in their art. The motivation of these artists may not have been to spread a false image but rather to show a group characterized as strong and powerful, done through the imagery of animal horned helmets and ornamental battle gear.[11]

The imagery in the art of this era has carried through to the modern day and influenced current conceptions, taken to be factual rather than symbolic representations.

But, the artifact that seems to have become the most widely associated with Vikings in reality does not actually appear to be connected to them. No evidence of Viking battle helmets adorned with animal horns has ever been found at archeological sites. Whether these types of helmets existed for ceremonial

---

10   Craig Bessell, "4 Major Misconceptions About Vikings," History Hit, last modified October, 2018, https://www.historyhit.com/major-misconceptions-about-vikings/

11   Johnni Langer. "The Origins of the Imaginary Viking." Viking Heritage Magazine 4, no. 2 (2002): 7-9.

purposes within the Norse culture is still widely contended. Instead, evidence suggests Vikings either went into battle bareheaded, or wore basic conical shaped metal, wood, and leather helmets with the occasional face shield. [12] For a group well versed in warfare and skilled in close combat, horned helmets would have been more of a hindrance in battle than any help, as the large protrusions would make for easier removal or create a larger target for weapon blows. [13]

The image of a female Viking warrior is also one that seems to permeate modern media, but evidence for the female warrior up until this point has been very sparse. Whether archeological findings of Vikings have been misinterpreted through a gender bias has been brought into question. Specifically with the discovery of a genetically female high status warrior, previously presumed to be male, at a Viking grave site in what is now present day Sweden has raised concerns about the way archeologists interpret findings. Given that many of the Viking warrior remains are identified as such based on the artifacts and clothing buried with the individual, and warriorhood is generally presumed to be a solely masculine pursuit, it is possible that other female warriors have been wrongly gendered based on these prejudicial criteria rather than on any genetic basis. [14] However,

12   Ryan Goodrich, "Viking History: Facts & Myths," Live Science, last modified August, 2018, https://www.livescience.com/32087-viking-history-facts-myths.html

13   Doug Ray, "7 Misconceptions About the Vikings That Might Surprise You," The Franklin Institute, last modified August, 2018, https://www.fi.edu/blog/viking-misconceptions

14   Neil Price et al. " Viking Warrior Women? Reassessing Birka Chamber Grave Bj.158." Antiquity 93, no. 367 (2019): 181-198.

despite these concerns, the existence of Viking women is still believed to be very rare. Rather it is more widely agreed that within the Norse culture the women's responsibilities were on the homeland where they were expected to take over the duties of the farms when the men left on these expeditions.[15]

Some modern day conceptions of the Vikings also include ideas of a barbarian nature, of being unkempt and unclean. But the numerous beauty items found at archeological sites suggest that the Norse people actually took hygiene and grooming very seriously, perhaps even more seriously than their European counterparts. Evidence of tweezers and combs made of wood and bone that do not greatly differ from modern versions of these same beauty items have been found on numerous occasions in Norse grooming kits. The hair of both men and women was well kept and regularly groomed. The idea that these people were all blonde is also not entirely true. Genetic research shows that vikings from Sweden were predominantly blonde, however Vikings from Denmark were predominantly red haired. Markings on the teeth of the Norse people also suggest tooth picks were commonly used to maintain some sort of oral hygiene.[16]

15   "Women in the Viking Age," National Museum of Denmark, n.d., https://en.natmus.dk/historical-knowledge/denmark/prehistoric-period-un-til-1050-ad/the-viking-age/the-people/women/

16   "What Did the Vikings Look Like?" National Museum of Denmark, n.d., https://en.natmus.dk/historical-knowledge/denmark/prehistoric-peri-od-until-1050-ad/the-viking-age/the-people/appearance/

You may have, at one time or another, heard someone refer to a Viking funeral and meant to set a dead body adrift on a burning boat out to sea. Though the Norse people had a variety of rituals for the dead, dependent on status, wealth, gender, and age, a Viking funeral in the sense mentioned above was not one of them. Viking ships were time consuming to build and costly. It would have been extremely impractical to set them alight for the sake of a theatrical funeral. Instead, within Norse culture it was more common that the dead were either buried in large burial mounds with various material items or were cremated in funeral pyres.[17]

---

17   Eleanor Barraclough, "10 myths About the Vikings," Oxford University Press Blog, last modified October, 2016, https://blog.oup.com/2016/10/ten-myths-vikings/

Scandinavian Geography and the Old Norse Language

The Vikings originated in a land we now call Scandinavia: a region in Northern Europe, composed of the kingdoms of Norway, Denmark, and Sweden. The Viking Age lasted from about 800 CE to 1050 CE, making the end of the era nearly one thousand years ago. Unsurprisingly, geographical borders today look much different than they did during the Viking age. The Vikings from Norway and Denmark went far overseas, while those from Sweden focused most of their efforts on eastward expansion across Europe. While the inhabitants of these three countries are culturally distinct, they have many close cultural ties. These ties will be explored in depth in the following chapters.

Foreigners also sometimes use the terms *Scandinavia* and *Nordic countries* interchangeably. The latter is actually a broad umbrella term that includes the Faroe Islands, Åland Islands, Finland, Iceland, and Greenland. The Faroe Islands, Åland Islands, and Finland have been populated by culturally-distinct peoples for millenia and do not share the same characteristics that are common between the Danes, Swedes, and Norwegian Vikings. Iceland was a previously uninhabited land until it was settled by the Vikings, and Greenland was inhabited by the Dorset people until Icelandic and Norwegian Vikings arrived. Though the Norse only stayed in Greenland until the 15th century, it still belongs to the Kingdom of Denmark today, and as such is considered a Nordic country.

A people's culture is largely developed in response to their geography.[18] Scandinavian geography is deeply varied, with flat lowlands comprising much of Denmark, and vast fjords, mountains, and archipelagos throughout Sweden and Norway.[19] While some areas have high levels of precipitation and temperate winters, others are dry and have very cold winters,[20] making the growing season short and sufficient food production difficult. The deep fjords and complex waterways resulted in geographical isolation between communities in Scandinavia, thus self-sufficiency was exceptionally important.[21] The plethora of lakes and waterways leading to the sea made fishing a logical source of sustenance for most communities across the three kingdoms.[22] Waterways were so essential to the Scandinavian way of life that ship building and sailing were highly developed skills across all peoples.[23] This advanced seafaring knowledge made them the

18   Beñat Elortza Larrea, "Medieval Scandinavia: Power Dynamics in the Viking Age," Medievelists.net, last modified June, 2020, https://www.medieval-ists.net/2020/06/power-dynamics-viking-age/.

19   "Scandinavia," New World Encyclopedia, n.d., https://www.newworl-dencyclopedia.org/entry/Scandinavia.

20   "Scandinavia."

21   "Where did they come from?" The Jorvik Viking Centre, n.d., https://www.jorvikvikingcentre.co.uk/the-vikings/where-did-they-come-from/.

22   "Where did they come from?"

23   Elortza Larrea, "Medieval Scandinavia."

most advanced naval peoples at the time.

One of the main cultural aspects that tied the people of Denmark, Norway, and Sweden together was their language. The Vikings spoke Old Norse, a language with germanic roots. Today, Old Norse no longer exists but has instead morphed into the various regional languages of Icelandic, Norwegian, Swedish, and Danish. Even Old Norse would have had some minor regional variations at the time of the Viking Age, but they would have essentially differed only in the way different accents vary according to region in the English language.[24] For example, although Southern US English, Midwest US English, Scottish English, and Irish English all sound very different, speakers from these regions can all understand each other. The Icelandic language that is spoken today is the closest existing language to Old Norse. What we currently understand as Old Norse actually comes primarily from Icelandic records, as most of the surviving records come from this region.[25]

Though we call the language of the Vikings Old Norse, the Vikings themselves called their language *dönsk tunga*, meaning "the Danish tongue." They did not use the Roman alphabet; instead, a runic alphabet called the Elder Futhark was used. The Elder Futhark was composed of 24 runes, but by the 9th century, the runic alphabet was reduced to just 16 letters and henceforth became known as the Younger Futhark. Old Norse runes were composed of different combinations of straight lines, making them

24   Daniel McCoy, "The Old Norse Language and how to Learn it," n.d., https://norse-mythology.org/learn-old-norse/#:~:text=Old%20Norse%20 was%20the%20language,of%20Norse%20mythology%20were%20written.&text=Speakers%20of%20Old%20Norse%20all,tungu%2C%20%E2%80%9CDan-ish%20tongue.%E2%80%9D

25   McCoy, "The Old Norse Language."

easy to carve into hard surfaces such as bone, wood, and stone -
the most common writing surface materials used by the Norse.[26]

Archaeologists believe that most Scandinavians would
have been able to read runes, regardless of social class. Stones
with inscriptions were erected in public places, thus they were
clearly intended for a wide audience.[27] Wooden writing tablets
have also been found in rural archaeological sites, indicating
they were used frequently by farmers and peasant folk as an
educational tool. These tablets had a raised border and were filled
with wax that could be removed with a stylus made of antler.
While some Norse runic inscriptions have been discovered in
Scandinavia and areas of expansions dating from the 11th century
and earlier, most of what we know about the language is from
well-preserved records from Iceland. During the Viking Age,
runes were only used for the occasional short message, as the
culture was mainly oral.[28]

26   "Stories, Poems, and Literature from the Viking Age," Hurstwic, n.d.,
http://www.hurstwic.org/history/articles/literature/text/literature.htm
27   "Stories, Poems, and Literature."
28   "Stories, Poems, and Literature."

OLD NORSE POETRY

Yggdrasil shakes,
and shiver on high

The ancient limbs,
and the giant is loose;

To the head of Mim
does Othin give heed,

But the kinsman of
Surt shall slay him soon.

How fare the gods?
How fare the elves?

All Jotunheim
groans, the gods are at
council;

Loud roar the dwarfs
by the doors of stone,

The masters of the
rocks: would you know yet
more?

Now Garm howls
loud before Gnipahellir,

The fetters will burst,
and the wolf run free

Much do I know, and
more can see

Of the fate of the
gods, the mighty in fight.

- from Völuspá[29]

---

29   Henry Adams Bellows, The Poetic Edda: Volumes 1-2, (New Jersey:
Princeton University Press, 1936).

A discussion of Norse language would be incomplete without mentioning Old Norse poetry. More than just artistic expression and entertainment, poetry was intertwined with Old Norse religion, and poems themselves were believed to be gifts from the gods.[30] Poets themselves were also revered within Norse society and were often commissioned by chieftains and kings. Though runic inscriptions were used, much of the Norse culture and belief system was passed down through the generations through storytelling;[31] this was the primary way in which culture and history were kept alive, thus the sharing of poems orally was of high importance. Sadly, oral traditions often do not stand the test of time, and historians must rely on the written record to find clues about a given culture's belief system.

Though poetry was undoubtedly a very big part of Norse life for centuries, the earliest known surviving Old Norse poem today can be found on the Eggja runestone, which dates from between the 7th and 9th centuries.[32] Found in 1917 overlooking the town of Sogndal in Norway, it is inscribed in Elder Futhark and is composed of around 200 ruins. The stone itself covers a burial chamber containing several items, but no body. It is difficult to read, as weather has eroded many of the ruins over time, but it appears to tell the story of the death of the person for whom the tomb was created. The Eggja runestone is an example of a *rune poem*: an inscription on a monument that venerates a specific person.[33]

---

30   "Stories, Poems, and Literature."
31   "Stories, Poems, and Literature."
32   "Old Norse Poetry," Viking Archaeology, n.d., http://viking.archeurope.com/literature/old-norse-poetry/
33   "Stories, Poems, and Literature."

These poems are usually quite short and simple in style. The Eggja runestone breaks this pattern by using a slightly more complex style involving alliteration.

Another form of poetry is *skaldic poetry*, which describes the achievements of important, high status persons.[34] These are usually written during the lifetime of this person, and the author often identifies himself. Skaldic poems vary tremendously in style dependent on the author. The term *skald* can be translated to mean *poet*.[35] The most elaborate structure of this poem is called the drápa, which is a type of longform poem. Though most praised a living person, *erfikvæði poems*, or funeral poems, were sometimes written by a skald to praise a well-respected person after their death.[36] The final two forms of skaldic poetry are the *genealogical poems*, which describe the ancestry of the subject (usually claiming descendancy from the gods) and *ekphrastic poems*: poems that describe the mythological background of objects belonging to the person being venerated.[37] Skalds occasionally wrote parody poems that poked fun at someone, but slander was a very serious offence, and if the claims made by the skald proved to be untrue, the skald would face severe punishment.[38]

The final type of Old Norse poetry is called *Eddic poetry*, which is composed of stories about the exciting adventures of the

34   "Stories, Poems, and Literature."

35   "Skaldic Poetry," Viking Archaeology, n.d., http://viking.archeurope.com/literature/old-norse-poetry/skaldic-poetry/

36   "Skaldic Poetry," Viking Archaeology, n.d., http://viking.archeurope.com/literature/old-norse-poetry/skaldic-poetry/

37   "Skaldic Poetry," Viking Archaeology, n.d., http://viking.archeurope.com/literature/old-norse-poetry/skaldic-poetry/

38   "Skaldic Poetry," Viking Archaeology, n.d., http://viking.archeurope.com/literature/old-norse-poetry/skaldic-poetry/

Norse gods and historical heroes. The style of these poems is often fairly simple, and the author is anonymous.[39] Our understanding of Eddic poetry comes from two texts called the *Prose Edda* (or Younger Edda) and the *Poetic Edda* (or Elder Edda). The Prose Edda was compiled around the year 1220 CE by the famous Icelandic historian, poet, and politician, Snorri Sturluson. It appears to be designed as a textbook on poetry, as it compiles many stories and is annotated by Snorri. The poems reflect pagan, Old Norse beliefs, but at the time it was compiled, Iceland had been a Christian country for over two centuries. This Christian influence is apparent in some of the texts, indicating that Snorri made small changes to reflect his own Christian beliefs.[40]

The Prose Edda is composed of a prologue and three books: Gylfaginning, Skáldskaparmál, and Háttatal. Gylfaginning (Here Begins the Beguiling of Gylfi) is composed of Odinic poems that explain Norse mythology.[41] Skáldskaparmál (The Poesy of Skalds) continues on the mythological stories from the first book, but also teaches about skaldic poetry.[42] The final book, Háttatal (The Enumeration of Metres) is composed of three songs celebrating the life and feats of King Hákon and his father-in-law, Skúli Bárdsson.[43]

39   "Stories, Poems, and Literature."
40   Kimberley Lin, "Edda," Ancient History Encyclopedia, last modified March 21, 2017, https://www.ancient.eu/Edda/
41   Kimberley Lin, "Edda," Ancient History Encyclopedia, last modified March 21, 2017, https://www.ancient.eu/Edda/
42   Kimberley Lin, "Edda," Ancient History Encyclopedia, last modified March 21, 2017, https://www.ancient.eu/Edda/
43   Kimberley Lin, "Edda," Ancient History Encyclopedia, last modified March 21, 2017, https://www.ancient.eu/Edda/

The Poetic Edda, discovered in 1643, was written in 1270, about fifty years after Snorri compiled The Prose Edda. It is also commonly known as the *Codex Regius*.[44] Though written later, it contains some poetry that predates Snorri's Edda. Archaeologists and historians agree that both texts appear to be using sources from an unknown earlier manuscript.[45] Unlike the Prose Edda, the Poetic Edda is written entirely in verse - hence the name. It contains eleven mythological poems and twenty-one heroic poems. The first mythological poem is called Völuspá, or *The Prophecy of the Seeress*. This is one of the most important poems for understanding Norse religion, as it outlines the creation of the universe, gods, and mythological creatures, as well as a war that leads to the end of the cosmos.[46] Much of the knowledge about Old Norse religion discussed in the next chapter has been derived from the Codex Regius.

44 "Eddaic, or Eddic Poetry," Viking Archaeology, n.d., http://viking. archeurope.com/literature/old-norse-poetry/eddaic-poetry/

45 Kimberley Lin, "Edda," Ancient History Encyclopedia, last modified March 21, 2017, https://www.ancient.eu/Edda/

46 Kimberley Lin, "Edda," Ancient History Encyclopedia, last modified March 21, 2017, https://www.ancient.eu/Edda/

Norse Paganism and Art

Religion

"Religion is the sigh of the oppressed creature, the heart of a heartless world, and the soul of soulless conditions. It is the opium of the people."

Karl Marx, *Criticism of Hegel's "Philosophy of Right"*

Marx's words seem to resonate with nearly all cultures over time, including the Vikings. However, these groups were polytheistic and believed in many gods.[47] The Viking Age was a period of considerable religious change, especially in Scandinavia.[48] Yet the popular image of Vikings has remained as pagans with a hatred of the Christian church. As mentioned in the

47   McCoy, "The Viking Spirit"
48   Williams, "Viking Religion" BBC, 2011, http://www.bbc.co.uk/history/ancient/vikings/religion_01.shtml

introduction, Old Norse religion has been regularly associated with acts of violence towards Christian groups. However, most scholars today believe that Viking attacks on Christian churches had nothing to do with religion, but more to do with the fact that monasteries were typically both wealthy and poorly defended, making them an easy target for plunder.[49] Even today, Old Norse religion can often receive more negative associations than classical mythology,[50] and the impact of this belief system has carried on much longer than the Vikings' time.

"Looking back over the history of mythological research, I did not really find any line of development that could explain why this difference should have arisen – at least not before the 1930s. To discover such a line, I found it necessary to widen the perspective and bring in some fundamental ideas about history. Then it became clear that the Napoleonic Wars had provoked a split between the French and German nation even within historiography and historical identity. The conflict between Romans and Germanic peoples in the Migration Period became a parallel to the modern conflict."[51]

As Viking raiders settled alongside Christian neighbours in the British Isles, settlers would often take native wives.[52] This,

49   Williams, "Viking Religion" BBC, 2011, http://www.bbc.co.uk/history/ancient/vikings/religion_01.shtml

50   Andrén, Jennbert, Raudvere, "Old Norse religion in religion in long-term perspectives"

51   Andrén, Jennbert, Raudvere, "Old Norse religion in religion in long-term perspectives"

52   Williams, "Viking Religion" BBC, 2011, http://www.bbc.co.uk/history/ancient/vikings/religion_01.shtml

coupled with the influence of the Church, gradually brought about a complete conversion.[53] This chapter discusses details regarding Old Norse religion and its beliefs regarding aspects such as the afterlife and sorcery. This chapter will also discuss Old Norse art, including tattoos, wood, stone and metal art. Elements of Viking mythology are often present in artistic ornamentation, and that religious content would have been obvious to contemporary viewers.[54]

The most widely used Old Norse word for "god" was *áss* (pronounced "OWS"), or *æsir* (pronounced "EYE-seer") in the plural ("gods"). Its corresponding feminine form for "goddess" was *ásynja* (pronounced "ow-SIN-ya"), or *ásynjur* (pronounced "ow-SIN-yur") in the plural ("goddesses"). When referred to as a collective that included both gods and goddesses, the masculine plural *æsir* was used. These words are all derived from one of two Proto-Germanic roots: **ansaz*, "pole, beam, rafter," or **ansuz*, "life, vitality."[55]

As Old Norse religion was polytheistic, it's not very surprising that there was also a belief in multiple afterlife realms. However, the Vikings' religions did not seem to contain any formal doctrines concerning what happens to someone after death[56]. The pictures presented by archeology and old literary

---

53   Williams, "Viking Religion" BBC, 2011, http://www.bbc.co.uk/history/ancient/vikings/religion_01.shtml

54   Groeneveld, "Viking Art," Ancient History Encyclopedia, 2018

55   Andrén, Jennbert, Raudvere, "Old Norse religion in religion in long-term perspectives"

56   McCoy, "The Viking Spirit"

sources do present some patterns in the way Vikings conceived the afterlife. It was believed that warriors would go to Valhalla, the most famous spiritual otherworld found in Old Norse religion[57]. This was the resplendent hall of the god Odin, and those chosen by Odin and his Valkyries would live there as celebrated heroes until called upon to fight by Odin's side in the doomed battle of Ragnarok[58].

Norse mythology is considered as a chronological set of tales, and the story of Ragnarok comes at the very end. Ragnarok comes from the Old Norse *Ragnarök*, meaning "fate of the gods." For the Vikings, the myth of Ragnarok was a prophecy of what was to come at some unspecified and unknown time in the future, but it had profound ramifications for how the Vikings understood the world in their own time[59]. The prophecy is that someday there shall come a Great Winter, unlike any the world has seen beforehand, causing mankind to become so desperate for food and other necessities of life. The loss would cause laws and morals to wear thin and fall away, and it would be an age of swords and axes[60].

"The wolves Skoll and Hati, who have hunted the sun and the moon through the skies since the beginning of time, will at last catch their prey. The stars, too, will disappear, leaving nothing but a black void in the heavens. Yggdrasil, the great tree that holds the cosmos together, will tremble, and all the trees and even the

57   McCoy, "The Viking Spirit"
58   McCoy, "The Viking Spirit"
59   McCoy, "The Viking Spirit"
60   McCoy, "The Viking Spirit"

mountains will fall to the ground. The chain that has been holding back the monstrous wolf Fenrir will snap, and the beast will run free. Jormungand, the mighty serpent who dwells at the bottom of the ocean and encircles the land, will rise from the depths, spilling the seas over all the earth as he makes landfall."[61]

The prophecy goes on to describe the gods going into battle, resulting in the cataclysmic destruction of the cosmos and everything in it. The battle would take place called Vigrid meaning "plain where battle surges".[62] The remains of the world would sink into the sea, and there would be nothing left but the void, causing creation to become completely undone[63], and some consider this the end of the tale. Others believe that a new world would arise out of the waters, as a man and a woman would have hidden themselves from the cataclysm in a place called the "Wood of Hoddminir[64].

In some cases, Old Norse religion presented shamans who did sorcery. A *völva* was considered a practitioner of magical tradition known as *seior*, and would wander from town to town prophesying and performing acts of magic in exchange for room, board, and other forms of compensation[65]. The most detailed account of this is presented in *The Saga of Erik the Red*[66], which offers accounts of the first Viking visits to North America and will be discussed further in this book.

---

61   McCoy, "The Viking Spirit"

62   Byatt, "Ragnarok: The End of the Gods"

63   McCoy, "The Viking Spirit"

64   McCoy, "The Viking Spirit"

65   McCoy, "The Viking Spirit"

66   Gritton, "Viking Age art styles: a key to the past," 2017.

Art

Viking art is a major reminder that common representations of Vikings are somewhat one-dimensional. We know that Vikings excelled as warriors, sailors, and explorers, as well as exceptional boat builders. Ships were often decorated with abstract, animal forms[67]. Art depicts other aspects of a Viking culture of storytellers, poets, artisans and artists. Viking art is commonly known as Norse art, and took on many forms, one of which was tattoos. Though some consider this mere speculation, a clue to confirm this possibility is an account from Ahmed Iban Fadlan in the year 921, when he was sent to Middle Volga, part of what is now Russia[68]. While there, he came across a group of Northmen and accounts that their skin was decorated with trees and other pictures[69]. However, beyond this, finding concrete evidence of this information is nearly impossible.

Evidence has been drawn that Vikings excelled at woodwork and metalwork, and were masters of a wide range of crafts such as jewellery, pottery, carving[70]. The art styles show roots of a traditional German animal ornamentation tracing back to the 4th

67   Gritton, "Viking Age art styles: a key to the past," 2017

68   Gazal, "When the Arabs met the Vikings," 2015, https://www.then-ational.ae/world/when-the-arabs-met-the-vikings-new-discovery-suggests-ancient-links-1.125718

69   Gazal, "When the Arabs met the Vikings," 2015, https://www.then-ational.ae/world/when-the-arabs-met-the-vikings-new-discovery-suggests-ancient-links-1.125718

70   Gritton, "Viking Age art styles: a key to the past," 2017

century[71]. There have been numerous reported cases of Viking-period stone sculptures in the United Kingdom, and museums around the world showcase artifacts from the Viking age. There are even cases of secular stone portraits, a type of artifact nonexistent before the Viking period, showcasing a warrior theme[72]. The popularity of the warrior theme in the 10th century reflects an assertion of aristocratic military ideals, which can also often be depicted through what remains of Viking art[73].

There is a fascination with Viking art, possibly due to its limitations and uncertainties. The wonder of how Vikings truly lived draws in many individuals. Gunnar Anderrson, Senior Curator at The Swedish History Museum states, "I think that the reason why our exhibition has been such a huge success so far is that we're telling new stories to each familiar theme that is in other Viking exhibitions as well." The museum's Viking exhibit has attracted more than 1.3 million visitors worldwide[74]. Gunnar describes two artifacts found in the exhibition: a Thor's hammer pendant made from silver and what is generally referred to as the oldest known crucifix in Scandinavia, also made from silver[75]. Each artifact contains exquisite detail and ornamentation in traditional tracing.

71   Gritton, "Viking Age art styles: a key to the past," 2017
72   Bailey, "Scandanavian Myth on Viking-period Stone Sculpture in England"
73   Bailey, "Scandanavian Myth on Viking-period Stone Sculpture in England"
74   "Vikings," Canadian Museum of History, 2016, https://www.history-museum.ca/vikings/
75   "Vikings," Canadian Museum of History, 2016, https://www.history-museum.ca/vikings/

We can draw the conclusion that Viking culture incorporated art into many aspects of Viking life. In 1902, Haakon Shetelig, a Norwegian archaeologist unearthed the most significant Viking burial mound ever discovered, featuring a full-fledged Viking longship in Oseberg, Norway[76]. Images of the ship show it decorated with intricate carvings. In comparison, rarer, pictorial art often seems to match known stories about Norse mythology, depicting such scenes as a Valkyrie welcoming a warrior into Valhalla[77].

It is worth noting the key characteristics of differing Viking age art styles, as styles do vary according to age. The following characterizations are drawn from Jim Gritton's *Viking Age Art Styles: Keys to the Past*.

Oseberg – This style is said to mark the full establishment of the Viking Age, showcasing semi-naturalistic, gripping beast motifs and sinuous animal forms. This style is best known by the wood carvings on the ship burial found at Oseberg.

Borre – Overlaps with Oseberg and Jellinge which notionally follows it. Featuring gripping beasts continues, usually

---

76   Ashworth, "Scientist of the Day: Haakon Shetelig," 2019, https://www.lindahall.org/haakon-shetelig/

77   Groeneveld, "Viking Art," Ancient History Encyclopedia, 2018, https://www.ancient.eu/Viking_Art/

depicted alone. Symmetrical interlaced patterns are typical of this style, which spread from Norse regions to the British Isles, appearing on metal and stonework.

Jelling – Emerged at the onset of the 10th century and is closely related to Borre. It is characterized by ribbon and S-shaped animals. Animal heads are usually depicted in profile.

Mammen – Evolved from Jelling style and was prominent in the early 11th century. This style features naturalistic lions, birds, serpents and leaf-like patterns.

Ringerike – Emerged in the early 11th century from an area north of Oslo where carvings on sandstones were discovered. Lions are often depicted, as well as plant motifs and leaf-like patterns.

Urnes – This style coincides with the end of the Viking age and takes its name from carved wooden panels on Stave church at Urnes, Norway. It features animals with almond-shaped eyes in complex, interlaced patterns. Designs are seldom symmetrical and it is not uncommon for animals to be depicted biting each other.

Society and Politics

The Viking lifestyle complimented relatively smaller groups of people than commonly found in society today, and throughout much of the Viking Age, specifically the earlier periods, political power lay in the hands of chieftains – warlords who ruled a relatively small group[78]. *Where is Vinland?:* an online Canadian library of source documents and virtual collections of archeological artifacts, states that a chieftain society differs from a state in that it has no central government and is instead ruled by several, even many chieftains or lords, each having his own domain of influence. These chieftains led the Viking expansion across Europe, commencing what is now known as the Viking Age. In order for a chieftain to maintain his power, he must gain followers willing to support him in armed conflict.

Vikings became chieftains through their wealth, skill in battle, and ability to command respect[79]. Chieftains often increased their power by defeating other chieftains in battle

---

78   McCoy, "The Viking Spirit"
79   Richardson, "Life of the Ancient Vikings"

across the land[80]. Erik the Red was one such chieftain who took his followers to Greenland to increase his wealth and status, and will be discussed further in this book. *Where is Vinland?* states that taxes were paid directly to the chieftain, and that chieftain societies are competitive and often unstable. This instability may have even played a role in the abandonment of Greenland and Vinland.

Chieftain societies are rarely stable. Inherent in them is a constant competition for power by the chieftains. Competition between chieftains became the downfall of both Iceland and Greenland. By the 13th century power was divided among just a few chieftains fighting each other. To gain the upper hand one chieftain signed away his own independence and that of the whole country by allying himself with the Norwegian king. As a consequence, the Norwegian crown gained the economic monopoly over Iceland in 1262 to 1264. This later led to an economic decline when Norway lost interest and ability to promote the well-being of Icelanders, yet still demanded taxes from them. Such a situation continued until 1944 when Iceland declared independence.[81]

In spite of instability, Viking societies did have three distinct social groups: the upper, middle, and lower classes—also known as Jarls, Karls, and Thralls (Mierswa, 2017). Upward mobility was possible for Karls but not Thralls (Mark, 2018). <u>Viking Jarls of</u>ten wore silk and expensive jewelry (Mark, 2018).

80   Richardson, "Life of the Ancient Vikings"
81   "Where is Vinland?", Great Unsolved Mysteries in Canadian History, last modified March 2007

Women were able to move up or down the heretical system and could improve their standing by jointly managing farmland with her husband and by exercising control over the land he had left to trade or work remotely, and most women who did so were Jarls, or members of the upper class[82].

Slavery was a prominent aspect of Viking culture and a large motivation for raids. Viking raiders captured slaves from all across Europe, including many women[83]. Male slaveholders had sexual access to their slaves, and often purchased women for that purpose alone[84]. It is believed that a man could declare any offspring an heir, but was not obliged to do so, and it was likely heirs would come from marriages[85]. The son of a slave woman can receive his rights due him if his father has acknowledged and freed him[86].

Women within the Viking cultures, however, had relatively greater freedom than in most other cultures at the time. Women were able to inherit property, own businesses, and divorce husbands[87]. The picture of women in Viking society is nowhere near complete, but there is evidence of women taking part in Viking expeditions and are perceived as having a hand in trade[88]. Women could also take on the role of a spiritual leader that

---

82   Mierswa, "Women Traders of the Viking Age"
83   Karras, "Concubinage and Slavery in the Viking Age"
84   Karras, "Concubinage and Slavery in the Viking Age"
85   Karras, "Concubinage and Slavery in the Viking Age"
86   Karras, "Concubinage and Slavery in the Viking Age"
87   Mierswa, "Women Traders of the Viking Age"
88   Mierswa, "Women Traders of the Viking Age"

inherited prophecies of Odin and Freyja, the preeminent goddess in Norse mythology[89].

There are records of Vikings participating in sports as well as organized festivals. Sports included mock-combat, wrestling, mountain climbing, swimming, javelin-throwing, hunting, a spectacle known as horse-fighting whose details are unclear, and a field game known as *Knattleik* which was similar to hockey[90]. Many traveled far distances to religious festivals, family celebrations and markets[91]. To keep followers happy, chieftains held feats in their halls and served meat, beer and mead, an alcoholic drink made from honey[92]. There would always be music, singing, and storytelling at the festivals, and some historians believe that the Vikings sometimes wore animal masks during the entertainment[93]. Though popularly imagined horned helmets were not used in battle, they were occasionally worn for ceremonial purposes (Mark, 2018). Sports and festivals often go hand in hand, and wrestling matches during the Viking era were no different, appearing to be duel-like and were fought to the death[94].

There were a variety of professions available for Vikings during this era. Most Scandinavians were farmers, but there were also blacksmiths, armorers, brewers, merchants, weavers,

89   McCoy, "The Viking Spirit"

90   Mark, "Vikings," Ancient History Encyclopedia, 2018, https://www.ancient.eu/Vikings/

91   Roesdahl, Else, Williams, Kirsten, Margeson, Susan, "The Vikings"

92   Richardson, "Life of the Ancient Vikings"

93   Richardson, "Life of the Ancient Vikings"

94   Short, "Games and Sports in the Viking Age," Hurstwic, 2009, http://www.hurstwic.org/history/articles/daily_living/text/games_and_sports.htm

luthiers (those who made stringed instruments), drum-makers, poets, musicians, craftsmen, carpenters, jewelers, and many other occupations[95]. Vikings participated in a significant amber trade, as amber, the fossilized resin of the pine tree, was considered a luxury good and was widely available in the Baltic region[96]. The amber trade was a significant source of income, and frequently washed up on the shores around Scandinavia[97]. It was worked into jewelry or sold in semi-processed form, especially to the Roman and Byzantine empires.[98]

Viking traders obtained these goods from locals, sometimes through trade, sometimes through force, and transported them to markets farther south, such as Bulgur or Kiev—or even all the way to Constantinople or Baghdad—where these goods were not available locally. In return, Viking traders would obtain silver coins, silk, glass, and other manufactured items that they could not produce themselves.[99]

95   Mark, "Vikings," Ancient History Encyclopedia, 2018, https://www. ancient.eu/Vikings/

96   "Environment and Trade," Khan Academy, 2019, https://www. khanacademy.org/humanities/world-history/medieval-times/environ-ment-and-trade/a/environment-and-trade-viking-age

97   Mark, "Vikings," Ancient History Encyclopedia, 2018, https://www. ancient.eu/Vikings/

98   Mark, "Vikings," Ancient History Encyclopedia, 2018, https://www. ancient.eu/Vikings/

99   "Environment and Trade," Khan Academy, 2019, https://www. khanacademy.org/humanities/world-history/medieval-times/environ-ment-and-trade/a/environment-and-trade-viking-age

Gaining a more well-rounded idea of Viking culture requires a look further towards exploration, trade, raiding, and settlement. The next section of this book will describe the many details differentiating Viking explorations across the globe, while also providing insight on the many aspects of exploration.

Part Two:

Going Viking

Viking Expansion and Integration across the British Isles

The British Isles refers to the geographical area that is now known as the United Kingdom and the Republic of Ireland. The United Kingdom is composed of four countries: England, Scotland, Wales, and Northern Ireland. The Republic of Ireland is an independent country and is a member country of the European Union. In the time of the Vikings, a united kingdom did not exist. England was composed of seven separate kingdoms – called a heptarchy – and each had their own reigning Anglo-Saxon monarch. These kingdoms were called Northumbria, Mercia, East Anglia, Wessex, Essex, Sussex, and Kent.

At the beginning of the 8th century, the area we currently know as Scotland was ruled by an ethnic group known as the Picts. Despite the Kingdom of the Picts being one of the strongest and most prominent kingdoms in Britain at this time, by the 9th century, they had essentially disappeared and their kingdom was replaced with that of the Scots, creating the land of Alba, or Scotland. The Scots are descended from the Gaels, an ethnic group from Ireland who immigrated to Scotland during the 5th and 6th centuries, thus they were (and remain) distinct from the Picts, Anglo-Saxons, and Britons.

In the Viking Age, Wales was split into North Wales and West Wales, the latter of which is presently an English county called Cornwall. North and West Wales were further split up into tiny kingdoms with petty kings and were often in conflict with each other. Ireland was also split into several small territories and included Northern Uí Néill, Southern Uí Néill, Airgíalla, Ulaid, Connacht, Laigin, and Munster. Although many Irish kings claimed to be the High King of all of Ireland, none ever gained full control over the island, but Northern and Southern Uí Néill were considered the leading dynasties of the island.

ENGLAND

The Anglo-Saxon Chronicle provides most of our knowledge about Viking presence in England. This chronicle was essentially a record of events and began to be compiled in the year 890 by the ruler of the Kingdom of Wessex, King Alfred the Great. After Alfred's reign, it was continuously added to up until the mid-12th century.[100]

The first recorded Viking raid in England took place in 793 in Lindisfarne, an island off the east coast of Northern

---

100   Edward James, "Overview: The Vikings, 800 to 1066," BBC History, last modified March 29, 2011, http://www.bbc.co.uk/history/ancient/vikings/overview_vikings_01.shtml.

England. It is written in the Anglo-Saxon Chronicle (translated from Old English) as follows: "…on the sixth day before the ides of January, the woeful inroads of heathen men destroyed God's church in Lindisfarne island by fierce robbery and slaughter."[101] As the Vikings were not Christian, they had no qualms about attacking monasteries and churches. With holy relics made of exquisite metalwork and precious gems and very little defenses, these Christian holy sites were the perfect target.

For the first few decades following the event in Lindisfarne, Vikings would flee to their ships immediately following a raid and return to Scandinavia with their newly acquired fortunes, but by the 850s, this began to change. They stayed in Britain over the winters and ventured further inland.[102] By the 860s, they were assembling armies with the intention of conquest.[103] The Norsemen were here to stay. In 866, the Vikings captured a Northumbrian city called Eoforwīc and renamed it Jórvik (known today as York). This became the Viking capital of England. A line of Viking kings ruled from York until 954 when King Eirik Bloodaxe was killed and English earls took back York.[104]

In addition to creating The Anglo-Saxon Chronicle, King Alfred the Great is remembered for his efforts and winning battles against the Vikings in England. In 878, he defeated them at the

---

101   James, "Overview: The Vikings."
102   "Anglo-Saxon Chronicle 11th Century," The British Library, n.d., http://www.bl.uk/learning/timeline/item126532.html.
103   "Anglo-Saxon Chronicle 11th Century."
104   "The Vikings in Britain: A Brief History," Historical Association, last modified January 13, 2011, https://www.history.org.uk/primary/resource/3867/the-vikings-in-britain-a-brief-history.

Battle of Edington, following which the Viking leader Guthrum converted to Christianity. Guthrum and Alfred signed a treaty, splitting England into "Danish" territory and English territory, the former of which was known as "Danelaw."[105] London had also fallen under siege of the Vikings, but in 886, Alfred took it back for the Anglo-Saxons.

The Kingdom of England was finally created in 927, and Alfred the Great's grandson, Athelstan, became king of England. Vikings raids continued, however, and four Vikings actually became King of England in the early 11th century, the most prominent of which was King Cnut, who became the ruling monarch of both England and Denmark.[106]

In 1066, the Viking king Harald Hardrada invaded northern England but was defeated by the English king, Harold Godwinson who had marched north to meet him. In Godwinson's absence, William the Conqueror, Duke of Burgundy (France) invaded England, and upon defeating the Vikings, Godwinson turned his army back south to meet the Normans. William defeated him and became the next King of England. This marked the end of the Viking raids in England. However, after having been in Britain for nearly three centuries at this point, the Vikings were never truly defeated. King Harold Godwinson was himself the son of a Danish noblewoman, despite being considered the last Anglo-Saxon king. Intermarriage between the Norse and English had been going on for years, and even William himself was a descendent of the Vikings. Many British persons today have some Viking ancestry.

---

105   "Anglo-Saxon Chronicle 11th Century."
106   "The Vikings in Britain."

SCOTLAND

The details of Viking invasion and expansion in Scotland is much less known than in England, as there is an absence of historical records.[107] Some historians have attributed the disappearance of the Picts to the presence of Vikings in Northern Britain,[108] however this is misleading; while Pictish culture certainly disappeared, the people themselves did not. A Pict himself, Kenneth Mac Alpin became king of both Picts and Scots in 843 and effectively united both peoples. Together, they fought off the invading English and secured Scotland's borders. His kingdom also consistently fought off Viking invaders, moved the relics of St. Columba from Iona to Dunkeld for protection, and created the Stone of Destiny – a stone bench on which all subsequent monarchs of Scotland were crowned upon – as a symbol of his nation's power to inspire his people.[109] As Viking raids increased, the Picts and the Scots became even more unified against this outside threat. The Picts gradually adopted Scots culture, leading to the disappearance of their ways.[110]

Based on current archaeological evidence, Vikings are thought to have first made contact with the Shetlands and Orkney Islands, located off the North coast of Scotland.[111] These islands were home to the Picts at the time. Archaeological evidence also

107   James, "Overview: The Vikings."

108   James, "Overview: The Vikings."

109   Joshua J. Mark, ""Picts," Ancient History Encyclopedia, last modified December 18, 2014, https://www.ancient.eu/picts/.

110   Mark, ""Picts."

111   "The Vikings in Scotland."

shows that the islands were inhabited by roughly equal numbers of Norse men and women shortly after making the first contact, thus this initial foreign expedition may have focused on colonization rather than raiding.[112] However, like Lindisfarne in England, coastal raids began to take place, and the Holy Island of Iona was burned by Vikings in 802.

In the early 9th century and beyond, Viking raids primarily took place in Northern and Western coastal regions and islands of Scotland, which included the Northern and Western (Hebridean) Isles, Caithness, Sutherland, and Inverness.[113] Many place names within these geographical areas today have Norse origins. Integration into Scottish society came more easily than in other places, due to cultural similarities between the Scots and the Norse. Their languages were similar, and both placed a heavy emphasis on kinship. Farming and domestication practices were also quite similar. The relationship between the Vikings and the people of the Scottish Highlands had a lasting influence. Clan systems can be traced back to the Vikings, and the traditional blackhouse style of dwelling found in the highlands is also very similar to Norse building styles.

WALES

Like Scotland, the impact of Vikings in Wales is much less clear than that in England. The greatest written evidence for Viking presence in Wales can be found in the Sagas of Icelanders.

---

112   "The Vikings in Scotland."
113   "The Vikings in Scotland."

In the Jómsvíkinga Saga, a Viking marries a Welsh princess and inherits a Welsh kingdom. Other sagas describe the Welsh coast and geography in such accurate detail that it is undoubtedly clear the Vikings were familiar with the area.[114]

Archaeological evidence indicates that the Vikings mostly kept to Eastern England, but there is evidence that some Viking raids took place in Wales as well. In 852, King Cyngen of Powys was slain by the Vikings. Tensions remained high up until 914 when Vikings moved along the coast of Wales and devastated nearly everything in their path. Along their way, they captured the Welsh Bishop Cyfeilliog of the Kingdom of Ergyng but were eventually driven out by Saxons.

Irish records have also been used to show evidence of Vikings in Wales, primarily through historical municipal documents that list the names of citizens in Welsh towns.[115] Many of these names were Norse, thus Vikings clearly settled in Wales, despite there being no yet-discovered archaeology that points to permanent Norse settlements. While they may not have settled as extensively in Wales as they did in England, they certainly spent a considerable amount of time there, if for nothing more than a jumping-off point between Britain and Ireland.

IRELAND

The first raid in Ireland was recorded in 795 when the island of Rathlin – just off the north coast of Ireland – was

---

114   Claire Holmes and Keith Lilley, "Viking Swansea," City Witness, n.d., http://www.medievalswansea.ac.uk/en/context/viking-swansea/.

115   Holmes and Lilley, "Viking Swansea."

attacked by Norwegian Vikings. In 798, St. Patrick's Island was burned, as were countless monastic sites peppered along the coast of Ireland. Like in England, for the several decades Vikings came and went on only a few ships at a time, immediately returning home with their newfound fortune upon acquiring it.

By the 840s, they began building longphorts - coastal fortresses that housed their ships - and began to spend their winters there.[116] They also established more permanent settlements in Wicklow, Waterford, Wexford, Cork, Limerick, and Dublin. This meant that raiding was no longer a seasonal activity that the Irish could prepare themselves for over winter, but was rather a year-round threat. Many Irish-born were taken as slaves for their camps. However, staying sedentary in these longphorts made the Vikings more vulnerable, and in 845, King Niall Caille of Tara attacked and defeated the Vikings of Donegal.

Because the Irish were not united under one kingdom and were always in conflict with each other, and the Vikings were often in conflict with each other as well, both parties made alliances with members of the opposite group in complex attempts to gain more power and control over Ireland.[117] Political marriages took place between the Irish upper class and Viking Jarls and Karls. In 851, Danish Vikings arrived in Ireland and targeted the Norwegian Vikings. The conflict between these two groups ensued for a couple of years, with the Norwegians finally managing to defeat the Danes. Some have speculated that the Irish instigated

116   Emma Groeneveld, "The Vikings in Ireland," Ancient History Encyclopedia, last modified December 11, 2017, https://www.ancient.eu/article/1162/the-vikings-in-ireland/.

117   Groeneveld, "The Vikings in Ireland."

this conflict,[118] but regardless of the truth of this statement, it certainly gave them much-needed respite.

Vikings did not truly gain any lasting power over any territories in Ireland, unlike in England and Scotland. By the end of the 10th century, the Irish gained the upper hand. The Viking king of Dublin at the time, Amlaíb Cuarán, had plans to expand his territory and raised an army. He slaughtered endless Irish, going so far as to kill the king of Leinster. Upon entering the kingdom of Meath in 980, he was met with resistance by the king Mael Sechnaill mac Domnaill and was killed. The King of Meath invaded Dublin and forced not just Dublin, but all Viking territories to fall under Irish rule. Over the next several decades, similar shows of Viking resistance followed, but the Irish continued to win. Vikings became more and more integrated into Irish society from this point on.[119]

118   Groeneveld, "The Vikings in Ireland."
119   Groeneveld, "The Vikings in Ireland."

Westward Expansion into Europe, the Middle East and North Africa

For three centuries, beginning around the year 800 CE, Northwest Europe was exposed to Viking raids[120], leading to continued raids across Europe, the Middle East and North Africa. It is suspected that Vikings discovered that great wealth could be gained from plundering the rich communities of the British Isles, and that eventually, economic interest in the British Isles and Northern Europe lowered, and opportunity for new wealth and adventure remained for the Vikings. This chapter will describe Viking exploration and settlement in Europe, the Middle East, and North Africa based on historical records and Viking legend.

---

120   Sawyer, "Kings and Vikings"

EUROPE

Vikings gained more than physical goods from European raids. It was in Western Europe that Vikings learned techniques to equip their boats with masts, eventually leading to the mastering of sailing and creating the possibility of long sea ventures[121].

Key countries to note when considering Viking exploration in Europe are France, Russia and the Byzantine Empire. Though Vikings were, for the most part, unable to achieve settlement in France during the well-defended Carolingian Empire, sporadic raiding did occur until the end of the Viking period[122]. The eastern Viking expansion was a relatively less violent process than the raids occurring in Western Europe and the British Isles, and the most prominent country in this area was Russia[123].

Rus are ancient people from whom Russia eventually gained its name, and though their origin and identity are still under dispute today, traditional western scholars believe them to have been Scandinavian Vikings[124]. Russian scholars,

---

121   Sawyer, "Kings and Vikings"

122   Editors of the Encyclopedia Britannica, "Vikings," Britannica, 2019, https://www.britannica.com/topic/Viking-people

123   Editors of the Encyclopedia Britannica, "Vikings," Britannica, 2019, https://www.britannica.com/topic/Viking-people

124   Tikkanen, "Rus," Britannica, 2015, https://www.britannica.com/topic/Rus

however, consider the Rus to be a southeastern Slavic tribe[125]. It is said that Vikings founded Kievan Rus in the mid-9th century by ruling over the Slavic tribes existing in the area[126]. This began with invasions of the Byzantine Empire ruled by Emperor Theophilus, the first marked appearance of Vikings in Europe[127]. Once Emperor Theophilus passed on and was replaced with his successor: Emperor Michael III, Vikings saw the opportunity for a major raid and attacked with a fleet of 200 ships[128]. It is stated that 20,000 Vikings surged ashore, and though the Emperor managed to prevent access to the capital just in time, the suburbs of the area were left unprotected[129].

Viking stories state that the region was initially divided and ruled by three brothers: Rurik, Sineus, and Truvor[130]. Rurik's brothers died within two years, so he claimed their territory and established Novgorod as the capital of his domain[131]. After Rurik died, his successor Prince Oleg of Novgorod captured the city of Kiev in 882 and moved the capital from Novgorod to Kiev[132].

125   Tikkanen, "Rus," Britannica, 2015, https://www.britannica.com/topic/Rus

126   Little, "When Viking Kings and Queens Ruled Medieval Russia," History Stories, 2019, https://www.history.com/news/vikings-in-russia-kiev-rus-varangians-prince-oleg

127   Tsouras, "The Fury of the Northmen," History Net, 2014, https://www.historynet.com/the-fury-of-the-northmen-viking-assault-constantinople

128   Tsouras, "The Fury of the Northmen," History Net, 2014, https://www.historynet.com/the-fury-of-the-northmen-viking-assault-constantinople

129   Tsouras, "The Fury of the Northmen," History Net, 2014, https://www.historynet.com/the-fury-of-the-northmen-viking-assault-constantinople

130   Little, "When Viking Kings and Queens Ruled Medieval Russia," History Stories, 2019, https://www.history.com/news/vikings-in-russia-kiev-rus-varangians-prince-oleg

131   Little, "When Viking Kings and Queens Ruled Medieval Russia," History Stories, 2019, https://www.history.com/news/vikings-in-russia-kiev-rus-varangians-prince-oleg

132   Little, "When Viking Kings and Queens Ruled Medieval Russia," His-

Opportunity for Vikings in Western Europe became very limited in the early 10th century, as fortifications had reduced the chance of quick results from raids, but a renewal of raids did still occur at times in Western Europe[133]. However, greater emphasis was placed on raiding the richer British Isles, and further exploration west, moving forward[134]. There are cases of famous Viking raids occurring in Spain, during the Vikings' initial attempts to push into the Mediterranean, the first being an attack of 100 ships on Gijon and Coruña in northern Spain[135]. This attack met firm resistance as the Muslim caliphate under Abd al-Rahman II fought back to achieve victory[136].

MIDDLE EAST

According to some reports, the Vikings carried on raiding Byzantine Empire settlements in the eastern

tory Stories, 2019, https://www.history.com/news/vikings-in-russia-kiev-rus-varangians-prince-oleg

133   Sawyer, "Kings and Vikings"

134   Sawyer, "Kings and Vikings"

135   Kinsella, "Russia, America and the Middle East: where did the Vikings visit to trade and raid?", History Extra, 2019, https://www.historyextra.com/period/viking/vikings-norse-raiders-where-countries-visit-impact-travell-russia-greenland-america-england/

136   Kinsella, "Russia, America and the Middle East: where did the Vikings visit to trade and raid?", History Extra, 2019, https://www.historyextra.com/period/viking/vikings-norse-raiders-where-countries-visit-impact-travell-russia-greenland-america-england/

Mediterranean[137]. The discovery of a silver ring with an Arabic inscription in a Viking grave has added credence to accounts of Arabic travelers in encounters with Norsemen, and points to a possible trade and cultural exchange[138]. "Contacts between Vikings and Arabic and Muslim people were both peaceful and violent. Since most of the contacts took place via trade, the relationship was mostly peaceful, but we also have accounts of Viking raids in the Caspian Sea which resemble accounts we have from Europe in a similar period," says Prof Hraundal Jonsson.[139]

Michael Crichton's 1976 novel *Eaters of the Dead, the 13th Warrior*, recounts the adventures of Ahmed Ibn Fahdlan, who encounters a band of twelve Viking warriors and joins their band as the thirteenth warrior. The book acts as a manuscript of Ibn Fadlan describing his experiences with the Vikings.
This manuscript represents the earliest known eyewitness account of Viking life and society, and portrays the Vikings quite differently than even traditional European views of these groups at the time[140]. The passage below was included in *Eaters of the Dead*'s introduction, and is said to be written by a twelve-century Irish writer:

137   Kinsella, "Russia, America and the Middle East: where did the Vikings visit to trade and raid?", History Extra, 2019, https://www.historyextra.com/period/viking/vikings-norse-raiders-where-countries-visit-impact-travell-russia-greenland-america-england/

138   Gazal, "When the Arabs met the Vikings," 2015, https://www.thenational.ae/world/when-the-arabs-met-the-vikings-new-discovery-suggests-ancient-links-1.125718

139   Gazal, "When the Arabs met the Vikings," 2015, https://www.thenational.ae/world/when-the-arabs-met-the-vikings-new-discovery-suggests-ancient-links-1.125718

140   Crichton, "Eaters of the Dead: The 13th Warrior"

In a word, although there were a hundred hard-steeled iron heads on one neck, and a hundred sharp, ready, cool, never rusting, brazen tongues in each head, and a hundred garrulous, loud, unceasing voices from each tongue, they could not recount of narrate, enumerate or tell, what all the Irish suffered in common, both men and women, laity and clergy, old and young, noble and ignoble, of the hardships and of injuring and of oppression, in every house, from those valiant, wrathful, purely pagan people.[141]

Crichton's own words point out that Vikings were never a clear, unified group, and featured many differing characteristics. What Europeans saw were scattered and individual parties of seafarers who came from a vast geographical area—Scandinavia is larger than Portugal, Spain, and France combined—and who sailed from their feudal states for trade, piracy or both; the Vikings made little distinction[142].

There is little concrete evidence found that provides insight on the relationship between Vikings and those in the Middle East. The ring found at the Viking grave site is an artifact worth marvelling, as it is the only ring of this kind to be found, according to Professor Sebastian Warmlander, a biophysicist on the research team that published the findings in March 2015[143].

141   Crichton, "Eaters of the Dead: The 13th Warrior"

142   Crichton, "Eaters of the Dead: The 13th Warrior"

143   Gazal, "When the Arabs met the Vikings," 2015, https://www.then-ational.ae/world/when-the-arabs-met-the-vikings-new-discovery-suggests-ancient-links-1.125718

Warmlander states that "the ring may therefore constitute material evidence for direct interactions between Viking Age Scandinavia and the Islamic world".[144]

NORTH AFRICA

Famous Muslim historian and geographer Abu Abdullah al-Bakri mentions in his *Book of Roads and Kingdoms* that the Vikings raided the city of Nekor, located in modern day Rif, Morocco, supporting historical Viking presence in Morocco. Based on another set of historical records from the *Fragmentary Annals of Ireland*, we can learn that the Vikings have raided a part in the north of Morocco during the 860's, where they battled the Berber Kingdom of the Moors.[145]

Motivations for heading further south were likely caused by low economic interest in Northern Europe at the time, and the Vikings ended up in Morocco following the raids in Spain,[146] The *Fragmentary Annals of Ireland* tell of Viking

144   Gazal, "When the Arabs met the Vikings," 2015, https://www.then-ational.ae/world/when-the-arabs-met-the-vikings-new-discovery-suggests-an-cient-links-1.125718

145   Bouzboune, "The Viking Adventure in Morocco," Morocco World News, 2017, https://www.moroccoworldnews.com/2017/03/210206/history-vi-king-adventure-morocco/

146   Bouzboune, "The Viking Adventure in Morocco," Morocco World News, 2017, https://www.moroccoworldnews.com/2017/03/210206/history-vi-king-adventure-morocco/

raids on Morocco in the 860s, said to have led to the taking of a massive amount of North African captives[147]. The following passage has been taken from the work:

> *Their arrogance and their youthfulness incited them to voyage across the Cantabrian Ocean (i.e. the sea that is between Ireland and Spain) and they reached Spain, and they did many evil things in Spain, both destroying and plundering. After that they proceeded across the Gaditanean Straits (i.e. the place where the Irish Sea [sic] goes into the surrounding ocean), so that they reached Africa, and they waged war against the Mauritanians, and made a great slaughter of the Mauritanians. There was hard fighting on both sides in this battle, and neither of them won the victory from the other in that battle. But all returned to camp, after many among them had been slain. However, they challenged each other to come to battle the next day.[148]*

The accounts have been viewed with some suspicion, as concrete evidence is limited. Nonetheless, the idea that Vikings raided along the coast of North Africa and captured and enslaved people from this region is supported by historical and archeological evidence.[149] The *Book of Roads and Kingdoms*, of course, also supports this idea.

---

147   Green, "A great host of captives? A note on Vikings in Morocco and Africans in early medieval Ireland and Britain," Dr. Caitlyn R. Green, 2015, https://www.caitlingreen.org/2015/09/a-great-host-of-captives.html

148   Radner, "The Fragmentary Annals of Ireland"

149   Green, "A great host of captives? A note on Vikings in Morocco and Africans in early medieval Ireland and Britain," Dr. Caitlyn R. Green, 2015, https://www.caitlingreen.org/2015/09/a-great-host-of-captives.html

Invasion and Settlement of Iceland and Greenland

There is relatively little known about the Vikings' North Atlantic exploration in comparison to European voyagers in the following century, but there is firm evidence of Vikings establishing settlements in both Iceland and Greenland. Norse expansion into the North Atlantic occurred between 800 and 1000 CE[150]. Viking history tells tales of sea-faring farmers who made the North Atlantic a Norse "lake" for one thousand years.[151] In the ninth century Vikings, mainly from Norway, began to colonize Iceland.[152] At the time, around the year 800, the Irish had also taken on seafaring and exploration, and had discovered Iceland[153]. There is speculation that Norse Vikings may have heard of the voyages of the Irish to Iceland and therefore sought this island in the north, but they might also have stumbled upon it accidentally. Another speculation is that Norsemen left their homeland in search of a place where their old customs and freedoms were not as threatened.[154]

150   Janzen, "The Norse in the North Atlantic," Heritage: Newfoundland and Labrador, 1997, https://www.heritage.nf.ca/articles/exploration/norse-north-atlantic.php

151   Fitzhugh, "Vikings: the North Atlantic Saga"

152   Dugmore, Keller, McGovern, "Norse Greenland Settlement: Reflections on Climate Change, Trade, and the Contrasting Fates of Human Settlements in the North Atlantic Islands"

153   "Vikings and Settlement," Icelandic Times, 2017, https://icelandic-times.com/132318/

154   Janzen, "The Norse in the North Atlantic," Heritage: Newfound-

There is no concrete evidence to provide a firm answer to the Vikings' motive for travel towards Iceland, other than the knowledge of Viking culture. However, we aren't left with nothing. Evidence of presence can be found in written records, particularly in Icelandic sagas as well as through some archaeological evidence, primarily L'Anse aux Meadows in Newfoundland. The following is a passage taken from the Icelandic Times published in 2017 mentioning three Vikings by name in written sources as explorers of Iceland:

The Viking Naddoddur is said to have been the first Norseman to come to Iceland and he did not find any sign of human habitation. He sailed back to Norway, calling the country Snæland ('Snowland'). Gardar Svavarsson, a Swedish Viking, sailed to Snæland. He was the first Nordic man to sail around the country, finding that it was an island. Consequently, he named it Garðarshólmur ('Gardarsholm'). He wintered at Húsavik on the Bay of Skjálfandaflói. Next spring when he was ready to sail back, he lost a boat from his ship with a man called Náttfari together with a man and woman slave. They settled in Reykjadalur. Therefore, Náttfari is the first Nordic man to settle in Iceland, but as he did not come to Iceland on his own initiative, he has not been included with the settlers. Flóki Vilgerðarson, a Norwegian Viking, sailed to Gardarsholm, intending to settle there. He therefore took with him his family and livestock. For guidance he took with him three ravens. When he released the first some way out, it flew back to Norway. When the second was set free further out, it returned to the ship, but later when the third was released,

---

land and Labrador, 1997, https://www.heritage.nf.ca/articles/exploration/norse-north-atlantic.php

it flew straight ahead, directing its owner to Iceland. After that Flóki was called Hrafna-Flóki ('Raven- Flóki'). They sailed along the south coast and to the fjord Vatnsfjörður on the north coast of the Bay of Breiðifjörður. Here they spent the summer fishing without procuring any hay for the livestock, which consequently perished during the following winter. Next spring Flóki climbed a mountain to look around. He then had a view over a fjord filled with ice, giving Iceland its name.[155]

Iceland is recorded to have been discovered by the Norse in 874 CE and was fully occupied by 930 CE, but by 975 CE a major famine had struck, creating a growing interest to find new lands for further expansion.[156] This quote has been taken from William Fitzhugh's *Vikings: The North Atlantic saga*:

Iceland was the staging point for the final series of West-Viking expansions that led to Erik the Red's discovery and settlement of Greenland, and the extension of that effort further west into North Greenland, and then further west into North America. Recent archaeological work not only offers a window into the four-hundred-year span of Norse Greenland (985-1450); but also gives us exciting new information about Viking voyages to Vinland. Evidence for the latter is presented from cartography and archaeology and includes a reconstruction of the Viking site discovered at L'Anse aux Meadows in northern Newfoundland.[157]

---

155   "Vikings and Settlement," Icelandic Times, 2017, https://icelandic-times.com/132318/

156   Janzen, "The Norse in the North Atlantic," Heritage: Newfound-land and Labrador, 1997, https://www.heritage.nf.ca/articles/exploration/norse-north-atlantic.php

157   Fitzhugh, "Vikings: the North Atlantic Saga"

Migration to Greenland began in the late 10th century, at approximately 982 CE,[158] and included Erik the Red before he continued on to Vinland. These were the initial steps to discovering what is now Newfoundland. It is recorded that 300 settlements were established in southeastern Greenland, clustered into two major settlements: the Eastern Settlement and the Western Settlement,[159] which were respectively found on the lower east side of the land mass, and the northwestern coast beside the Davis Strait.[160] The Eastern Settlement was older and larger, while the Western Settlement was closer to northern hunting grounds and never had a population greater than 1,000-5,000.[161]

Motivation for Norse settlement in Greenland is predicted to be a desire for a balance of trade and subsistence.[162] A written account of Erik the Red and the naming of Greenland, can be found in Íslendingabók (the Book of the Icelanders), a short

158   Janzen, "The Norse in the North Atlantic," Heritage: Newfoundland and Labrador, 1997, https://www.heritage.nf.ca/articles/exploration/norse-north-atlantic.php

159   Janzen, "The Norse in the North Atlantic," Heritage: Newfoundland and Labrador, 1997, https://www.heritage.nf.ca/articles/exploration/norse-north-atlantic.php

160   Kintisch, "The Lost Norse: Why did Greenland's Vikings disappear?", Science Mag, 2016, https://www.sciencemag.org/news/2016/11/why-did-greenland-s-vikings-disappear

161   Janzen, "The Norse in the North Atlantic," Heritage: Newfoundland and Labrador, 1997, https://www.heritage.nf.ca/articles/exploration/norse-north-atlantic.php

162   Dugmore, Keller, McGovern, "Norse Greenland Settlement: Reflections on Climate Change, Trade, and the Contrasting Fates of Human Settlements in the North Atlantic Islands"

chronicle of Iceland's early history. by Ari Þorgilsson the Learned. The story is told below:

> *The land which is called Greenland was discovered and settled from Iceland. Eirik the Red was the name of a Breidafjord man who went out from here and took land in settlement at the place which has ever since been called Eiriksfjord. He gave the land a name, and called it Greenland, arguing that men would go there if the land had a good name.*[163]

However, settlement on Greenland was not permanent and the question remains today: why did the Vikings of Greenland disappear? Theories for the colony's failure have included Basque pirates and the black Plague, and so on, but historians have most often pinned large responsibility on the Vikings and their difficulty to adapt to the changing climate.[164] With the local onset of cooler conditions, the increasing extent of pack ice could have seriously affected shipping and compromised hunts for marine mammals, in particular forays into the northern hunting grounds for walrus.[165] Hand in hand with the development of more extensive pack ice, the shortened growing seasons, reduced fodder production, longer over-wintering periods, environmental degradation, and more demanding conditions for raising domestic animals could have made the subsistence

163   Karlsson, "The Natural History of Iceland"

164   Kintisch, "The Lost Norse: Why did Greenland's Vikings disappear?", Science Mag, 2016, https://www.sciencemag.org/news/2016/11/why-did-greenland-s-vikings-disappear

165   Dugmore, Keller, McGovern, "Norse Greenland Settlement: Reflections on Climate Change, Trade, and the Contrasting Fates of Human Settlements in the North Atlantic Islands"

base of the Norse more precarious than it had been at the time of settlement[166] The last documented Viking contact with Greenland was 1409 CE.[167]

Nonetheless, Viking's settlement in Iceland and Greenland was essential in the story of North American exploration and the settlement of Vinland. During the nearly five centuries the Norse were in Greenland, they inevitably came into contact with North America.[168] Archeological evidence has been uncovered at multiple locations, one of the most famous being L'Anse aux Meadowssettlement in what is now Newfoundland. L'Anse aux Meadows shows that many elements of the Vinland sagas are factual, in particular Lief Erikson's saga version of the settlement. This continuation of exploration and discovery, as well as Leif Erikson's saga, will be the focus of the following section of this book.

166   Dugmore, Keller, McGovern, "Norse Greenland Settlement: Reflections on Climate Change, Trade, and the Contrasting Fates of Human Settlements in the North Atlantic Islands"

167   Dugmore, Keller, McGovern, "Norse Greenland Settlement: Reflections on Climate Change, Trade, and the Contrasting Fates of Human Settlements in the North Atlantic Islands"

168   Wallace, "Leif Eriksson"

Part Three:

Writing about Vinland

The Sagas of Icelanders

Before archaeologists found physical evidence for Viking presence in North America in 1960, there was already speculation that Icelanders and Greenlanders had set foot on the east coast of Canada and the United States. This supposition came from historical written records, chiefly a couple stories in the collection of Sagas of Icelanders. The Norse word *saga* means *tale* or *story,* thus the Sagas of Icelanders are stories written about some of the first inhabitants of Iceland. The events within these stories take place between the 9th and 12th centuries, however, they remained oral stories until the 13th century, during which they were transcribed onto parchment. While historians are fairly certain that most, if not all, were composed within this century, many only exist today in their 14th and 15th century copies.

Unlike the Eddic poems that tell tales of the exciting adventures and exploits of the Norse gods, and the heroic achievements of historic Norse kings and warriors, the Sagas of Icelanders tell the stories of the fairly common Norse men and women who settled Iceland,[169] and later Greenland. The sagas are

---

169   "Stories, Poems, and Literature."

unique in the respect that they contain a higher degree of accuracy than many sources from other cultures of the time. Though the events and details within the sagas should be treated cautiously when used in an academic setting, there are several tools that scholars can employ to check the accuracy of many of these stories. Several of these methods have been used to verify the events told in the two sagas that mention the discovery of Vinland: the Graenlendinga Saga (Saga of Greenlanders) and Eiriks Saga Rauda (Saga of Erik the Red).

In the introduction, the story of the Celtic queen Boudica was used as an example of how bias is present in written records - even within authors of events contemporary to their own lifetime. Not even an eyewitness account can be free from bias. The historian's job is to determine the extent to which details of events have been modified, added, or removed, and to what extent the author's own biases may have contributed to the content of the final manuscript. Understanding what the perspective behind the author's biases is also important. Oftentimes, these questions cannot be fully answered and the success that historians have in answering them changes on a case by case basis.

At the time the sagas were written, Icelanders had been converted Christians for roughly 200 years, and the influence of Christianity can be seen in many of the sagas. Though the discovery of Vinland took place right around the time that Christianity was becoming widespread in Iceland, some of the sagas took place prior to the Christianization of Iceland. Despite this, some stories are told through the lens of the Christian belief system, making it quite clear that the authors would have changed certain aspects to fit their worldview. According to Cormack, most historians agree that the sagas do provide valuable and accurate "insight into the social structure and social processes of Iceland," but these structures and processes are reflective of the 12th and 13th centuries in which they were written, rather that the structures and processes on the 9th, 10th, and 11th centuries during which the stories and take place.[170]

An example of this can be seen in the portrayal of certain events in the Saga of Erik the Red. Although most men on the expedition to Vinland are Christian, one man is not. He asks Thor to help the men find food, and a whale washes up on shore - seemingly delivered by Thor. When the men eat it, they fall ill, and upon repenting to God for consuming a gift from a pagan deity, they are rewarded with an abundance of food sources. A little further into the tale, this same man is blown off course from his destination, ends up in Ireland, and is killed - the predictable fate of a heathen pagan.

It is also largely unknown who wrote the sagas, and whether each one has a single author or several. It is likely that the surviving manuscripts have been edited by multiple authors over many years.[171] There are likely multiple versions of each[172] of the eighty or so sagas that survive to this day, though whether each surviving manuscript has only been copied from previous works a couple of times, or fifty times, is unknown. None of the original manuscripts from the 13th century survive. Each subsequent author may have taken liberties and changed details to reflect their

---

170   Margaret Cormack, "Fact and Fiction in the Icelandic Sagas," History Compass 5, 1 (2007): 207. https://doi.org/10.1111/j.1478-0542.2006.00363.x.

171   "Stories, Poems, and Literature."

172   Cormack, "Fact and Fiction."

own ideas about how the story should be told.[173] These ideas may have come from some other written, reliable source, but they also may be due to a family's own belief in the validity of their own rendition of the story, or for political motivations. Despite these biases, many historians agree that the sagas still contain a high degree of accuracy.

The first clue is cultural. During the Viking Age, the exaggeration of facts about a person or event was generally unheard of, as doing so was considered mockery.[174] The Norse perceived mocking to be so insulting that the mocker could actually be punished with death for spreading such lies.[175] For this reason, the sagas - and the Skaldic poems - are understood to be fairly reliable accounts of people, at least intentionally so. However, oral traditions cannot be tracked, and some details may be unintentionally exaggerated.[176] Thus, the details do need to be treated cautiously.

Though a couple hundred years seems substantial, in historical terms it is a relatively short period of time, and an oral tradition that tells stories over this length of time is likely to still retain a considerable degree of accuracy. Writing itself began to become more widespread around the same time that Iceland converted to Christianity, and even if the sagas themselves were not being written, various details about the events in them may have been written down in some other form. Thus, though the

173   Cormack, "Fact and Fiction."

174   "Stories, Poems, and Literature."

175   "Stories, Poems, and Literature."

176   Gréta Sigríður Einarsdóttir, "A Guide to Reading the Sagas of the Icelanders," What's On, n.d., https://www.whatson.is/guide-reading-sagas-ice-landers/

Saga of Greenlanders and the Saga of Erik the Red were written two centuries after the first explorations to Vinland took place, they are likely to be minimally modified. All scholars concur that the sagas contain real people and events, but agreement on what proportion is factual events, and what proportion is invention, is much harder to reach.[177]

To determine the historical accuracy of a saga, supporting evidence must be used to validate the words on the page.[178] There are some similarities between other texts from other parts of the world and the sagas, such as the *Anglo-Saxon Chronicle* and Adam of Bremen's *Gesta Hammaburgensis Ecclesiae Pontificum*, both of which which outline events in the lives of Sveinn Forkbeard and Olaf Tryggvason. The sagas tell the same stories of these individuals, albeit in greater detail.[179]

Archaeological evidence has been used to prove and disprove the accuracy of the sagas as well. Cormack uses the example of an archaeological excavation that was prompted by Egils Saga, in which the description of Egill Skallagrimsson within the text seems to indicate that he may have had Paget's disease. This prompted the excavation of the location where his bones were said to have been put to rest and revealed many pieces of evidence that corroborated assertions made in the saga.

In the following two chapters, the two sagas that deal with Vinland will be summarized, and although their accounts of events differ in some ways, the differences and similarities between the

---

177   Cormack, "Fact and Fiction."
178   Cormack, "Fact and Fiction."
179   Cormack, "Fact and Fiction."

two are very useful in determining the historical content from the narrative. Leif Erikson is the first person to set foot on Vinland in both sagas, but the sister of Leif, Freydis, is portrayed in two very different ways. In Eiriks Saga Rauda, she scares away the Indigenous people who attack the Norse, but in the Graenlendinga Saga, she organizes the expedition, murders her partners, and then murders her partners' wives. The differing depiction of women and gender highlights how important it is to keep the context of the social and political structures of the sagas in mind.[180]

Similarly, the physical evidence found along the east coast of North America corroborates many events in the Graenlendinga Saga and Eiriks Saga Rauda. The sagas may be the key to finding further archaeological evidence of Norse exploration and activity in North America. While further physical evidence will be difficult to find, it is not impossible.

---

180   Cormack, "Fact and Fiction."

Eiriks Saga Rauda

Though the Saga of Erik the Red is mainly about Norse exploration in North America, ironically, Erik the Red did not join this expedition, nor is his life the centre of this saga. The original manuscript is believed to have been written during the 13th century, approximately 200 years after the events detailed in the story, but only two copies of the saga exist today. The earliest surviving version is within Hauksbók, dating from the early 14th century. This manuscript was composed by Hauk Erlendsson, a descendent of two characters in the story: Thorfinn Karlsefni and Gudrid. A second version can be found in Skálholtsbók, dating from the 15th century. The main difference between the two versions is that Hauk's is a little more specific and detailed. It is possible that he added information based on stories passed down in his family[181]. This saga also combines all the expeditions into one long, three-year expedition, whereas in the Saga of Greenlanders, there are multiple expeditions.

Erik the Red was the father of Leif Erikson, who became

---

181   "Erik the Red's Saga," Where is Vinland? Great Unsolved Mysteries in Canadian History, n.d. https://www.canadianmysteries.ca/sites/vinland/whereis-vinland/eriktheredsaga/indexen.html

the first Viking to set foot on North American soil. The saga begins by outlining the genealogy of a seemingly unrelated family to Eirik the Red. It pays special attention to Thorstein the Red, who conquered much of Scotland, including the areas of Caithness, Sutherland, Ross, and Moray. Eventually, the Scots rebelled against him and killed him. This chapter also mentions Thorstein's mother, Aud the Deep-Minded. Though there were not many Viking women, she may, by some definitions, be considered one of the few. Upon her son's death, she had a ship built in secret and then captained this ship to Iceland.

In the second chapter of the saga, we meet Erik the Red. Erik and his father, Thorvald, lived in Jadar, Norway, before being exiled to Iceland as punishment for committing manslaughter. Erik did not stay out of trouble in Iceland, and was again exiled. He travelled across Iceland looking for a place to settle with his people, and eventually left Iceland and sailed Greenland. Erik is credited with creating the first Norse settlement on Greenland. The names *Iceland* and *Greenland* seem as though they should be swapped; Iceland is really much greener than Greenland, and Greenland is much more icy than Iceland. However, Eirik named it so intentionally, saying "men will desire much more to go there if the land has a good name."[182]

A woman called Gudrid is introduced next, who is described as "the fairest of all women, and of peerless nobility in all her conduct."[183] She is sent to be fostered by a man called Orm, but when Orm advocates for the son of a skrall who wishes to propose to Gudrid, her father, Thorbjorn, is insulted and takes

182   John Sephton, "Translation of Eirik the Red's Saga," *Transactions of the Literary and Philosophical Society of Liverpool* 34 (1880): 183-212.

183   Sephton, "Translation of Eirik the Red's Saga."

Gudrid back into his care. Thorbjorn runs into financial troubles and decides to leave Iceland before his family becomes disgraced. He decides to settle in Greenland with his friend Erik the Red. Upon arriving in Greenland in the midst of a harsh winter, they are taken in by a man called Thorkill, and here a seeress makes a prophecy, telling Gudrid she will marry in Greenland, but the marriage will not last long and she will spend much of her life in Iceland. The weather improves, and they set off to Erik's settlement, who upon arrival gives Thorbjorn a large farmstead where he dwells for the rest of his life.

We learn of two of Erik's sons: Thorstein, who lives in Greenland with his father, and Leif, who serves King Olaf Tryggvason in Norway. After a period of service, the king sends Leif back to Greenland to spread Christianity. The seas are rough on his voyage to Greenland, and Leif and his crew come upon an unknown land, with "fields of wild wheat, and the vine-tree in full growth."[184] He finds men who have been shipwrecked and takes them back to Greenland with him, thereby giving him the name *Leif the Lucky*.

We hear a bit about Leif's attempts to spread Christianity, and though his father takes offense, his mother quickly converts and has a church built. She also becomes celibate, causing "a great trial to [Erik's] temper."[185] The land that Leif had come across on his trip to Greenland is a topic of interest, and an expedition is planned by Thorstein, Leif, and Erik. It does not go to plan, and they get lost at sea before returning home to Greenland.

---

184   Sephton, "Translation of Eirik the Red's Saga."
185   Sephton, "Translation of Eirik the Red's Saga."

Gudrid and Thorstein marry, but as the seeress prophesied, Thorstein becomes sick and dies. Her father also dies shortly after, leaving his estate to his daughter Gudrid. Erik takes Gudrid into his household. A new character enters the story at this point: Thorfinn Karlsefni, a man we know to be wealthy and from a good family, arrives in Greenland in the autumn with his company. He takes an interest in Gudrid, and they are married in the winter.

Vinland is soon made mention of again, and another expedition is arranged. Freydis, the daughter of Erik the Red, marries a man called Thorvard, who attends this expedition along with a longtime friend of Erik, Thorhall. Gudrid's new husband, Thorfinn, leads this expedition. The saga says that approximately 160 men were in their company, and that "most of them in this ship were Greenlanders."[186] The ship they take on this expedition is the ship that Thorbjorn and Gudrid had arrived on. As this ship is used consistently throughout the saga, it is likely they did not have others of this size and spent time repairing this one repeatedly.

This expedition proves to be much more successful. After two and a half days, they reach North American land. Exiting their boats, they explore it on foot and find that much of the land is covered in big, flat stones, so big that "two men might well lie on them stretched on their backs with heel to heel."[187] Also in abundance are "polar-foxes," which are likely meant to be Arctic Foxes. They call this place Helluland, which means stone-land.

---

186   Sephton, "Translation of Eirik the Red's Saga."
187   Sephton, "Translation of Eirik the Red's Saga."

Again, they sail for two and a half more days, heading south. They come across land that looks much different from Helluland, covered in trees and abundant in wildlife. On a little island south-east of this land, they find many bears and name it Bjarney, meaning Bear Island. The mainland they name Markland, meaning forest-land. Once again, they sail for two and a half days and come across land without a harbour but with lots of "long sandy strands."[188] The Vikings call this area Furdustrandir, meaning wonder-shore, on account of it being so difficult to navigate their ships through. Upon rowing to land, they find the keel of a ship. This part of the ship makes up the backbone of the ship, and runs along the center of the bottom of the ship from front to back. The fact that they come across this on North American land, where the Indigenous tribes living there do not build ships, is very interesting. Most likely, it washed up on shore after a wreck out at sea.

Creeks begin to appear along the coastline and they decide to sail their ship into one of these. On this expedition, they brought with them two Scots that King Olaf had sent back to Greenland with Leif. These Scots are named Haki and Haekja, and they send them out to find good land to settle upon. Three days later, Haki and Haekja return with grapes and wild wheat, and after boarding the ship, they direct them further south. They reach a firth, and directing the ship along it, they find an island in the middle of swirling currents (thus they name it Straums-ey, or stream-island). This island is described as having so many birds "that scarcely was it possible to put one's feet down for the eggs."[189] Continuing along the firth, they reach land and unload

---

188   Sephton, "Translation of Eirik the Red's Saga."
189   Sephton, "Translation of Eirik the Red's Saga."

their belongings and begin to set up a permanent base. The place is described as having mountains and being "fair to look upon,"[190] and they name it Straumsfjordr.

It is mentioned that they brought cattle with them, and Straumsfjordr offers large pastures. They decide to stay there for the winter, but the winter is severe, and they go hungry. After some time, a whale is driven to shore and they gladly harvest it to eat. Unfortunately, all the men fall ill upon consuming it. Here, the influence of Christianity in the sagas makes an appearance: Thorhall claims the whale was an answer to a prayer he had made to Thor. The rest of the men are Christian, and they throw away the whale meat and pray for God's forgiveness. Fishing is said to immediately improve, and they successfully hunt on the mainland and gather eggs from Straums-ey to supplement the fishing. Their prayers are answered by God.

That summer, Thorhall and Thorfinn go their separate ways: Thorhall decides to go North with a company of just nine men, and Thorfinn and the rest of the men decide to explore south and towards the east, hoping to find warmer weather. Unfortunately, Thorhall's ship gets blown off course, and he ends up all the way in Ireland, where the men are beaten, and Thorhall is killed.

Thorfinn has much better luck. Sailing south, they arrive at a river surrounded by several large islands, and at high tide, they are able to access the river and come upon a land which they call Hóp. As Thorfinn had hoped, this place is warmer and more abundant in food. There is wheat, vines, and rivulets full of

---

190   Sephton, "Translation of Eirik the Red's Saga."

fish - including halibut. Wild animals "of every form"[191] roam the forests; they do not want for food. They build dwellings around a lake along the river, as well as further inland.

After spending about a month in Hóp, they encounter the Indigenous people for the first time, waking one morning to find nine canoes. They decide to take a white shield with them, as a token of peace, and walk towards the water to meet these unknown people. The canoes moved to shore, and the saga describes these men as being short, with large eyes, broad cheeks, and messy hair. The Indigenous people looked upon the Vikings for a while before sailing off again.

Thorfinn and his men stay at Hóp for the winter, which is so mild that they do not have snow. When spring arrives, they encounter the Indigenous people again. This time, so many canoes are on the horizon that it looks "as if the sea [is] strewn with pieces of charcoal."[192] They trade with the Vikings, offering furs and hides for cloth. They also want to trade for the swords and lances of the Vikings, but Thorfinn thinks this would be unwise and refuses to make this trade. They called these unknown people *Skrælingar*.

One day, during a trade, an aggressive bull rushes out of the woods. This scares the Skrælingar back to their canoes, and the Vikings do not see them again for several weeks. When they return, they do not come peacefully. The Vikings take their red shields this time to meet them and they battle. The Skrælingar bring large poles with large balls the size of a sheep's stomach

191   Sephton, "Translation of Eirik the Red's Saga."
192   Sephton, "Translation of Eirik the Red's Saga."

attached to the ends, and the Vikings retreat. Freydis - who we do not know accompanied the men on this expedition until now - comes out and scolds the men for retreating. Freydis grabs a sword and bares her body to the Skrælingar, which scares them away. Two Vikings and four Skrælingar are killed in this confrontation.

Although Thorfinn thinks this newly discovered land is plentiful, he does not want to live with the threat of war looming over them. They begin to prepare to return to Greenland, but end up staying in North America longer than planned. Sailing towards the north, they come across five Skrælingar who appear to be outlaws and slaughter them. Going further north still, they arrive at Straumsfjordr, where Freydis decides to remain with a hundred men.

Thorfinn journeys south again and stays at Hóp for two months before setting out to find Thorhall, not knowing he had been blown off course to Ireland and is no longer in North America. They come across a "race of men that have only one foot,"[193] and conflict ensues. To avoid more violence, they continue north. Upon reaching Markland, they find five more Skrælingar: one man, two women, and two children. They capture the children, teach them the Old Norse language, and baptize them. They then take them back to Greenland where they live with Erik the Red, and Thorfinn returns to Iceland with Gudrid.

---

193   Sephton, "Translation of Eirik the Red's Saga."

The Graenlendinga Saga

There are two major detailed accounts of Viking visits to Vinland, both in the form of Norse sagas: *The Graenlendinga Saga* ("Saga of Greenlanders") and *Eiríks saga rauða* ("Erik the Red's Saga"). *The Graenlendinga Saga* was written in the 13th century but relays events in the late 10th and early 11th centuries, so validity is once again worth considering.

Like the Saga of Erik the Red, the Saga of Greenlanders begins by telling the story of Thorvald and Erik's exile to Iceland, and Erik's subsequent banishment that leads him to settle Greenland. However, while Erik the Red's saga describes intentional Norse exploration to Greenland and Leif's discovery of North America, *The Graenlendinga Saga* differs by describing Bjarni Herjólfsson as the first European to sight mainland North America when his Greenland-bound ship was blown off course westward, leading him to sail along the Atlantic coastline of eastern Canada before returning to Greenland.[194] Sigurd Stefansson's map of Vinland and other "-lands," which will be

---

194   Wallace, "Vinland," Britannica, 2016, https://www.britannica.com/place/Vinland#ref226391

discussed in the following chapters, features a legend reading "Island of Vínland discovered by Bjarni and Leif in company."[195]

Though Bjarni saw the North American coast by ship, it is recorded that he did not go ashore. It is suspected that the reason for this was out of caution, to not put his crew in any danger or heavily uncertain circumstances. Leif Erikson was inspired by Bjarni's tales of his journey, persuading him to travel to the North American coast and spend the winter in Vinland. Leif wishes his father, Erik, to lead the expedition, but Erik is reluctant and believes he is meant to stay in Greenland. Instead, Leif agrees to lead the first expedition to Vinland. This account differs from the saga of Erik the Red, wherein Thorfinn Karlsefni is the focus of the story rather than Leif.

Before arriving on Vinland's shore, Leif's expedition first came to an icy and barren land which he appropriately named Helluland or "Land of Flat Rocks."[196] After this while continuing south, the ship encountered a flat wooden land, which Leif named Markland or "Land of Forests."[197] Continuing south, the ship eventually reached a warmer, more hospitable area where they built a base named Leifsbúoir or "Leif's Camp."[198] In this area they found fine lumber and many wine grapes, leading to the naming of Vinland or "Land of Wine."

195   Seaver, "Maps, Myths, and Men"
196   Wallace, "Vinland," Britannica, 2016, https://www.britannica.com/place/Vinland#ref226391
197   Wallace, "Vinland," Britannica, 2016, https://www.britannica.com/place/Vinland#ref226391
198   Wallace, "Vinland," Britannica, 2016, https://www.britannica.com/place/Vinland#ref226391

The description of *Leif's Camp* marks another difference between the two sagas. In the Saga of Erik the Red, this place is not mentioned. Straumfjord is mentioned as the winter camp instead. Grapes are also not found in the winter camp, but are instead located further south at the site of Hóp. They stay in Leif's Camp over the winter, and in the spring return to Greenland with a ship full of grapes and lumber. They encounter a group of Norsemen who have been ship-wrecked and bring them back to Greenland.

The Saga of Erik the Red tells the tale of a single expedition to Greenland, lasting several years. The Saga of Greenlanders tells the story of not just Leif's initial expedition, but several subsequent ones. In the couple of years following Leif's journey, Vinland remains of much interest to the Greenlanders. Leif Erikson's brother, Thorvald, decides to lead a second expedition to Vinland. Thorvald takes only thirty men with him, and they settle at Leif's camp over the winter. In the spring, he decides to explore the surrounding areas. Going westward, he finds a cornshed, but no other evidence of human habitation. The following summer, he explores northeastward and comes upon a forested area. Nearby, they encounter the Skraelingar for the first time.[199]

There find nine Skraelingar hiding under three canoes, and capture all but one who manages to escape. Thorvald and

199   Wallace, "Vinland," Britannica, 2016, https://www.britannica.com/place/Vinland#ref226391

his men kill the eight they have caught, and explore the area further, finding what they believe to be dwellings. This marks another prominent difference between the sagas. Far from being peaceful, Thorvald's first encounter with the Skraelingar is violent. Thorfinn's first encounter in the Saga of Erik the Red is peaceful; the men approach the canoes with white shields raised, and many weeks of trade take place between the people until the Skraelingar are provoked by the attack of the Vikings' bull. In the Saga of Greenlanders, the Skraelingar are, justifiably, provoked by an outright attack, and the man who escapes returns with reinforcements and attacks Thorvald and his crew. Thorvald is fatally wounded in this attack, and after burying him in Vinland, his crew returns home to Greenland.

According to the Saga of Greenlanders, another expedition is planned to bring Thorvald's body back to Greenland.[200] Thorvald was Christian and his grave was marked with two crosses.[201] Thorstein, brother of Leif and Thorvald, takes a crew of 25 men and his wife, Gudrid, to Vinland. Unfortunately, they fail to find the new land and return to Greenland. Though this expedition is said to have failed, historians agree that it is very likely that his body was brought back to Greenland for burial at Brattahlid by one of the subsequent expeditions.[202] Upon

200   Wallace, "Vinland," Britannica, 2016, https://www.britannica.com/place/Vinland#ref226391
201   Wallace, "Vinland," Britannica, 2016, https://www.britannica.com/place/Vinland#ref226391
202   Wallace, "Vinland," Britannica, 2016, https://www.britannica.com/place/Vinland#ref226391

returning, Thorstein falls ill and like in the Saga of Erik the Red, he prophesies that Gudrid will remarry and return to Iceland.

The fourth expedition is led by Thorfinn Karlsefni, the hero of the Saga of Erik the Red. Thorfinn arrives in Greenland and falls in love with Gudrid; the two are married that winter. He sets off for Vinland with a crew of 60 men and five women, where upon arrival, they spend the winter in Leif's Camp. Here they make contact with the Skraelingar, who they make trades with. Like in the Saga of Erik the Red, the Skraelingar are interested not just in the red cloth and dairy products that the Vikings offer, but also in their weapons. Thorfinn does not allow the men to trade their weapons. During one of these trades, a Skraelingar tries to take one of the crew's swords, and the man slays him. The Skraelingar flee, but return in large numbers ready for attack. Here, the story follows a similar chain of events as the Saga of Erik the Red.

A fifth and final expedition is relayed in the Saga of Greenlanders. This expedition is led by Erik the Red's daughter, Freydis. She plans to voyage to Vinland with two brothers, Helgi and Finnbogi. The brothers arrive first and begin to set up their lodging in the great hall that Leif slept in. Upon Freydis' arrival, she demands they remove their belongings, as Leif gave her permission to stay in his hall, so the brothers build their own hall.

Over the winter, the two parties are constantly resolving small disputes that arise between them. When spring arrives,

Freydis decides she wishes to return to Greenland and meets with Finnbogi to discuss this. Finnbogi, wishing to resolve the disputes between them once and for all, offers to trade his large ship for Freydis' smaller ship so that she and her crew may return to Greenland while the brothers stay in Vinland a while longer.

Freydis agrees to this bargain, but double crosses the brothers. She claims that Finnbogi hit her and threatens to divorce her husband, Thorvald, unless he defends her. Her husband and the crew slay the brothers and their crew, sparing only their wives. Freydis refuses to let the women live and slays them herself, and then threatens to kill anyone who relays these events in Greenland. She returns home with both her share of the profits, and the profits of the brothers, and tells Leif that the brothers chose to stay behind. In the end, the truth comes out and Leif is livid.

Though these two sagas differ in a few major ways, both provide valuable clues to the archaeological search for evidence of Viking presence in Atlantic Canada. Though the site of L'Anse aux Meadows (which will be discussed in future chapters) is likely the winter camp that Leif built, and subsequent expeditions used as well, there are several details about this camp in the Saga of Greenlanders that do not fit the archaeological evidence. The site of Straumfjord in the saga of Erik the Red, and an alternate unknown summer site, seem to fit best. However, the description of multiple expeditions in the Saga of Greenlanders, as opposed to a single expedition in the Saga of Erik the Red, is also a better fit. Taken together, the sagas can be used to differentiate between literary elements and historical facts.

Descriptio Insularum Aquilonis and Other Records

Adam of Bremen was a German medieval chronicler who lived and worked in the later 11th century, and composed a candid "description of the islands of the north" which deals with Russia, the Baltics, Scandinavia, Iceland, Greenland, as well as the earliest known reference to Vinland.[203] This passage has been taken from his *Descriptio Insularum Aquilonis,* the oldest surviving record of Vinland, written in 1075:

He spoke of an island in that ocean discovered by many, which is called Vinland, for the reason that vines grow wild there, which yield the best of wine. Moreover than gran unsown grows there abundantly. Is not a fabulous fancy, but, from the accounts of the Danes, we know to be a fact. Beyond this island, it is said, that there is no habitable land in that ocean, but all those regions which are beyond are filled with insupportable ice and boundless gloom.[204]

203   Turville-Petre, "Germanic religion and mythology," Britannica, 2019, https://www.britannica.com/topic/Germanic-religion-and-mythology

204   Descriptio Insularum Aquilonis

It is recorded that Bremen was told of Vinland by Danish King Svend Estridsen. Knowledgeable in history and geography, Sweyn was Adam of Bremen's main source on Scandinavian affairs in the latter's valuable *Gesta Hammaburgensis ecclesiae pontificum*.[205] This work is supplemented by the ten accounts of Scandinavian history listed below that were written in Denmark, Norway and Iceland between the early twelfth and middle of the thirteenth century. The following passage describes King Sven's interesting story of his rise to power:

> *After the death of Canute in 1035, when Hardecanute was ruling in Denmark and Magnus in Norway, the young kings agreed that whoever lived longer would rule both countries. Under this agreement Magnus became king also of Denmark in 1042 and appointed Sweyn viceroy. While Magnus was fighting the Slavs in 1043, Sweyn, who was favoured by the Danish nobles, was acclaimed king, provoking a war over the Danish throne with Magnus and then with his successor, Harald III Hardaade.*[206]

Adam of Bremen's work falls into a unique class, not only because it is the only work contemporary with King Sven, but also because Adam had actually met and known Sven personally. This, of course, has the potential to create biases within the work

205   The Editors of Encyclopedia Britannica, "Sweyn II Estridsen: King of Denmark," Britannica, 2007, https://www.britannica.com/biography/Sweyn-II-Estridsen

206   The Editors of Encyclopedia Britannica, "Sweyn II Estridsen: King of Denmark," Britannica, 2007, https://www.britannica.com/biography/Sweyn-II-Estridsen

and should be acknowledged by those seeking a true glimpse into the Viking era. Furthermore, it is important to note that Adam's work has influenced subsequent history works created during the 12th and 13th centuries, most containing information acquired from Adam's work, however modified in order to serve the different intentions of the authors.[207]

There are three maps that display what we perceive today as Vinland, though it is not certain that their information is factual. However, each map placed the location of Vinland around Chesapeake Bay in 1570. Sigurd Stefansson's map of Vinland and other "-lands" is the most well-known and referenced map in this case, and positions Vinland at the same latitude as England and Ireland.

The Vinland map depicts a long narrow peninsula called extending toward the north, lying south of *Markland* and *Helluland* and opposite *Skrælingeland*. Sigurdur's original map has been lost, but what survives is a copy made in 1690 for Thordur Thorlaksson, also known by his Latinized name, Thorlacius, another Bishop of Skálholt.[208] Thordur added comments in the margin. The map is featured in the collections of the Danish Royal Library.[209] A second map was made in 1605 by Hans Poulsen Resen, who had a vivid interest in

207   Sawyer, "Kings and Vikings"

208   "Where is Vinland?", https://www.canadianmysteries.ca/sites/vinland/othermysteries/maps/indexen.html

209   "Where is Vinland?", https://www.canadianmysteries.ca/sites/vinland/othermysteries/maps/indexen.html

Iceland and its ancient history.[210] Resen worked as professor at the University of Copenhagen, and his map was made shortly after a Danish expedition to Greenland in the summer of 1605 to search for the Norse settlements there.[211] This map also shows Vinland as a long narrow peninsula extending north.

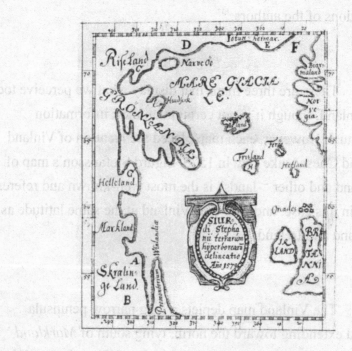

The map is a small black and white map executed on parchment depicting a large island in the far northwestern Atlantic, identified by two Latin legends beside it as Vinilanda Insula, giving the map its name.[212] Translated into English, the legend reads "Island of Vínland discovered by Bjarni and Leif in company."[213] The only "Bjarni" mentioned in the *Saga of Eirik the Red* is a man named Bjarni Grimolfsson, a man so devoted to his father that he sailed to Greenland to find him and his voyage

210   "Where is Vinland?", https://www.canadianmysteries.ca/sites/vinland/othermysteries/maps/indexen.html

211   "Where is Vinland?", https://www.canadianmysteries.ca/sites/vinland/othermysteries/maps/indexen.html

212   Seaver, "Maps Myths, and Men: The Story of the Vinland Map"

213   Seaver, "Maps Myths, and Men: The Story of the Vinland Map"

reached the American coast before making his way back to Greenland to find his father's new farm.[214] This leads us to believe that the Bjarni mentioned is Bjarni Herjólfsson, whose story holds key familiarities with Grimolfsson's.

Iclandic chronicles over the years, including Charles Sprague Smith's *The Vinland Voyages* (1892), mention Vinland and Markland from up to 1347. Thus, contact with North America seems to have continued much beyond Leif Erikson's lifetime. *The Vinland Voyages* also state that King Olad Tryggvason sent Leif Erikson to Greenland to proclaim the faith there, which was what led Leif to find Vinland the Good. Though thxxxe written record of Viking expansion is relatively limited in comparison to those proceeding it, a combination of written and archaeological evidence helps to focus the blurry image of Vikings and the Viking Age. The next section of the book will provide archaeological evidence coinciding with the written evidence found from this era.[215]

214   Seaver, "Maps Myths, and Men: The Story of the Vinland Map"
215   Sigurd Stefansson, Manuscript Department, Royal Library, Copenhagen, retrieved from https://www.canadianmysteries.ca/sites/vinland/othermysteries/maps/indexen.html

Part Four:

The Archaeological Evidence

L'Anse aux Meadows

Part Four

The Archaeological

In 1960, the little community along the Médée Bay lived off the fishing industry. A French fishing station had existed along this bay from the 18th century up until 1904, and the little hamlet was given the name L'Anse à la Médée, or Medea's Cove, to reflect their close proximity to and reliance on the little picturesque bay that would have once been covered in trees. Though the station closed in 1904, the fishing economy continued on a smaller scale for the next several decades. The French influence diminished, and the hamlet began to be called *L'Anse aux Meadows*. Although the villagers often set their sights northward off the coast of the very tip of Newfoundland and across the ocean beyond, those strange grass-covered mounds south of Médée Bay remained in the back of their minds.

Next to Médée Bay, you'll find Islands Bay - formerly known as Epaves Bay, within the Straight of Belle Isle. It's along this bay that the local peoples found the grass mounds. The most southerly one was very large, with two tiny mounds on each end of its south-eastern edges. A little ways further north there was another sizable mound, smaller than that first southerly one, but still big enough to be noticed. North of this were another two tiny mounds, but spaced further apart. Finally, north of this was the last mound. This final mound was the largest by far, and almost as wide as it was long.

Although the inhabitants of L'Anse aux Meadows have undoubtedly speculated about these mounds for centuries, it wasn't until William Munn published his speculations that those "Indian burial mounds" might actually be the remains of a Norse site in 1914 that interest was truly generated.[216] This publication in a St. John's newspaper, called *The Evening Telegram*, sparked international curiosity. A Finnish geologist, Väinö Tanner, made the same induction as William Munn in 1939, and in 1956 a Danish archaeologist, Jørgen Meldgaard, planned to undertake a full excavation, but was delayed by other projects.[217] The interest of all these specialists across the world piqued the interest of these humble villagers further, and when a Norwegian explorer by the name of Helge Ingstad arrived in 1960, local George Decker took him to the mounds to see what he thought.[218]

It just so happened that Ingstad's wife was an archaeologist, and, interest ignited, Anne Stine Ingstad led the first full excavation of L'Anse aux Meadows between the years of 1961 and 1968. The amount of archaeological material found was staggering, and the locals musing were answered once and for all: the site was, without a doubt, a Viking settlement. Radiocarbon dating indicated that it had last been inhabited by

216   Birgitta Wallace, "L'Anse aux Meadows," The Canadian Encyclopedia, last modified March 2, 2018, https://www.thecanadianencyclopedia.ca/en/article/lanse-aux-meadows

217   Wallace, "L'Anse aux Meadows."

218   Wallace, "L'Anse aux Meadows."

the Norse in the 11th century - 500 years prior to the arrival of Christopher Columbus.

It has now been about sixty years since L'Anse aux Meadows was discovered, yet it remains to be the earliest known archaeological evidence of European activity in all of North America, and the only known Norse settlement across the Atlantic.[219] Excavated copper mines along Lake Superior indicate that millions of pounds of copper were extracted during the bronze age - 2000 to 4500 years before L'Anse aux Meadows was occupied - yet only a miniscule percentage of this can be accounted for amongst Native American artifacts. Some archaeologists and historians have suggested that the Minoan people of Santorini and Crete travelled across the Atlantic to harvest copper to be brought back to their own Empire.[220] Although this proposition is compelling, definitive proof does not yet (and may never) exist, thus L'Anse aux Meadows remains significant as the earliest evidence of Europeans on North American soil.

While the Norse may have been the first Europeans to set foot in what is now known as Canada, they were certainly not the first to occupy the site. Five distinct Indigenous groups occupied it prior to Viking occupation, and one more occupied it again after the Norse had abandoned it. The Vikings who arrived on the shores of Canada would have known that they were not the first, as they would have been able to see the remains of a hearth

219   "L'Anse aux Meadows National Historic Site," United Nations Educational, Scientific, and Cultural Organization [UNESCO], n.d., https://whc.unesco.org/en/list/4/

220   Gavin Menzies, The Lost Empire of Atlantis, (New York: William Morrow Paperbacks, 2012).

and tent rings.[221] A group of Indigenous persons known as the *Cow Head tradition* would have occupied sites in the vicinity at this time: these would have been the skraelings that the Vikings mentioned in the sagas.

As the sagas indicate, the Vikings never intended to permanently settle on the shores of Newfoundland. Archaeological evidence indicates that the site was occupied around the year 1000 CE, but only for a relatively short period of time - approximately ten years.[222] There are certain key elements that archaeologists look at when deciding whether a site was intended for long term, colonized use, or whether it was meant as a temporary base. One such key indicator is whether there is presence of animal activity. If barns or livestock artifacts are present at a site, the people may have intended to build a farmstead. L'Anse aux Meadows shows no such evidence.[223] The lack of evidence for cattle is compelling, as the sagas indicate that the Vikings brought cattle with them from Greenland.

Though permanent settlement was never a goal, the archaeological evidence at the site still tells an interesting tale. In total, eight buildings were excavated, all of which were built with wooden frames and covered in a turf roof made of peat. The style of these buildings is consistent with the popular styles in Iceland and Greenland around the year 1000 CE.[224] A peatbog is located nearby and would have been used as the source for the roofing.

---

221   Wallace, "L'Anse aux Meadows."
222   Wallace, "L'Anse aux Meadows."
223   Wallace, "L'Anse aux Meadows."
224   "L'Anse aux Meadows National Historic Site."

The three largest mounds were all halls. The most northerly, largest hall would have housed the leader of the expedition. It was twice the size of Erik the Red's Greenlandia home, and equal in size to chieftain halls in Iceland.[225] It had a private sleeping area, a massive common area for banquets, a couple gigantic storage rooms, and a lean-to shed for housing boats in need of repair. The most southerly hall is also significant in size and would have housed persons of a high social status. Like the largest hall, it had private and common living quarters, as well as slag that indicates iron working. The hall between the two was the smallest and is likely to have housed laborers.[226] It had one shared living space in addition to a storeroom.

Red jasper flints, used for starting fires, were found in all three halls and provide insight into the home countries of the inhabitants. Most of the flints in the smaller two halls are made of Jasper from Iceland, but the flints in the largest hall are made from Jasper from Greenland. The dating of the artifacts indicates that all of these buildings would have been occupied at the same time. Many of the 800 artifacts are wood chips, smelting slag, and wood planks and nails from ships.[227] It is clear from the abundance of these artifacts that the Vikings at this site were constantly busy with ironwork and woodwork, probably to repair their ships.[228] In a smaller quantity were the small personal items that were likely lost by their owner. These included a ringed pin, which would have been used as a fastening on a cloak, a tool used for making

225   "L'Anse aux Meadows National Historic Site: Maps and Brochures," Parks Canada, Government of Canada, last modified March 30, 2017, https://www.pc.gc.ca/en/lhn-nhs/nl/meadows/visit/cartes-maps

226   "Maps and Brochures."

227   Wallace, "L'Anse aux Meadows."

228   "L'Anse aux Meadows National Historic Site."

cloth called a spindle wheel, a whetstone used for sharpening blades, a hair pin, a gilded ring, and a glass bead.

The artifacts indicate that most of the Vikings at L'Anse aux Meadows would have been men, though the spindle whorl and hair pin suggest some women would have also been present. The site likely supported somewhere between 70 and 90 Norse, and the stark differences in the buildings are evidence that they were from varied social classes.[229] While this number of persons may sound low, it was actually substantial. It would have taken up to two months to build the site, and the Norse population of Greenland around the year 1000 CE was approximately 400,[230] meaning that Greenland would have given up over 17 percent of its population to embark upon this expedition. While they didn't intend to settle, they certainly found the coasts of Canada to be of high value.

Though L'Anse aux Meadows is the only Viking settlement to yet be discovered, the archaeology here shows that the Vikings explored other areas along the coast. Though the majority of the jasper flints are from Greenland and a smaller proportion from Iceland, a couple aren't from either. The remaining two are from Notre Dame Bay - in Newfoundland.[231] This bay is located a considerable ways south from L'Anse aux Meadows, along the east coast of Newfoundland. Some of the wood chips found were made of linden, and butternut wood and butternuts themselves were also found at the site. None of these are native to the area, however.[232] They only grow as far east as

229   Wallace, "L'Anse aux Meadows."
230   Wallace, "L'Anse aux Meadows."
231   Wallace, "L'Anse aux Meadows."
232   Wallace, "L'Anse aux Meadows."

New Brunswick; thus, there is evidence that the Vikings travelled at least this far south and west as well.

When these archaeological findings are compared with the details in the sagas, we find several details are confirmed. First, the size of the northerly hall and the Greenlandia jasper flints indicate that Leif Erikson would have lived within this hall during his time in Canada. As there appear to be no attempts at colonizing, it seems clear that, like the sagas outline, the Vikings would have placed value on Vinland due to its abundance of lumber, furs, nuts, and grapes. While the butternuts would have grown in New Brunswick, so too would the Vikings have come across an abundance of grapes alongside those butternuts. This is very likely why they called it *Vinland* - the land of wine.

However, we also learn from the sagas that the Vikings spent their summers on a site abundant in grapes, so according to the sagas, L'Anse aux Meadows cannot be the place they called Hóp - their summer camp. It does, however, fit the definition of the settlement referred to as Straumfjord in Eiriks Saga Rauda - the winter camp. This camp was also called Leifsbuxir, translated as "Leif's Camp," mentioned in the Graenlendinga Saga.[233] This is more evidence that Leif Erikson would have lived in the largest hall at L'Anse aux Meadows.

While archaeologists are fairly certain that L'Anse aux Meadows is in fact a winter camp from which the Norse would have ventured out from to explore, one glaring question remains: where is the archaeological evidence for the settlement of Hóp?

233   Birgitta Wallace, "Norse Voyages," The Canadian Encyclopedia, last modified February 7, 2016. https://www.thecanadianencyclopedia.ca/en/article/norse-voyages

Hóp, Helluland, and Markland

Though many of the events in the saga of Erik the Red take place at the settlement of Hóp (meaning *lagoon*), there is no archaeological proof of it to this day. Archaeologists have speculated about where it might be located without much luck. What they do know is that the settlement referred to as Leifsbudir in the Saga of Greenlanders is likely the site at L'Anse aux Meadows. Some archaeologists also think that it may also be the site of Straumfjord in the Saga of Erik the Red, but others think Straumfjord, and the nearby island of Straums-ey, refer to another unknown location.

Archaeologists and geographers have also pinpointed the locations of Helluland and Markland. Helluland, or stone-land, is believed to refer to the geographical area from Baffin Island (located almost directly westward from Erik the Red's Greenland settlement of Brattahlid) off the coast of Nunavut down to the Torngat Mountains in Northern Newfoundland and Labrador. Baffin Island is home to arctic foxes, which were described as being plentiful in Helluland. This island would have been inhabited during the time of Viking exploration. These people would have likely been the late-Dorset people, who went extinct between the year 1000 CE and 1500 CE.

Patricia Sutherland theorizes that the Viking explorers and the Dorset people may have made contact. While this view is controversial, the evidence is compelling. A soapstone bowl was discovered at a site near the community of Kimmirut in the 1960s, dating from around the year 1000 CE. It was originally believed to be a Dorset artifact, but recent research indicates that this bowl is actually a crucible: a tool for melting metal for metalworking.[234] The Dorset people of this time did not practice metalworking; they would have heated copper to bend it slightly, but smelting was only done in Europe at this time.[235] Whetstones, used for sharpening blades, and tally sticks, were also found at this site, further supporting the assertion that metalworking was being done at Kimmirut.

In 1984, a 3-metre segment of yarn was found in Pond Inlet on Baffin Island, dating from the 13th century.[236] Though some have argued that the Dorset people could have figured out how to make yarn, as it is not a complicated process, similar yarn skeins have been found at the site of Nuuk in Greenland and date from the same century. The Dorset people wore clothing that was sewn from animal skins. Despite the controversy over which culture is responsible for manufacturing the yarn, when looked

234   Sarah Rogers, "Metalworking Tool Suggests Evidence of Medieval Europeans on Baffin," Nunatsiaq News, January 9, 2015. https://nunatsiaq.com/stories/article/65674metalworking_tool_suggests_evidence_of_medieval_europeans_on_Baffin/

235   Sarah Rogers, "Metalworking Tool."

236   Jane George, "Archeologist Identifies Viking Artifact near Pond Inlet," Nunatsiaq News, December 3, 1999. https://nunatsiaq.com/stories/article/archeologist_identifies_viking_artifact_near_pond_inlet/

at in conjunction with other artifacts, the presence of Vikings on Baffin Island seems entirely plausible.

The site of Tanfield Valley also provides some clues. Rat pellet fragments matching Old World rats from Europe have been found, which may have come from rats on Viking ships.[237] Other artifacts include a whalebone shovel, similar to the kind used in Greenland to cut sod, cut stones resembling those that were cut using European masonry, and stone ruins similar to ruins of Viking buildings in Greenland.[238] Though the site had previously been determined to be much older than the time period during which Vikings were in North America, the site may have been occupied across multiple time periods. Altogether, the archaeological evidence on Baffin Island indicates that the Greenlanders and Dorset people had an ongoing trade network between them.

Markland, the Land of Forests, is believed to refer to a large region around the Hamilton Inlet in central Labrador.[239] The taiga, or boreal forest, is abundant in this area. To date, there has not been any archaeological evidence of temporary Viking settlement in this area. It is likely that the Vikings would have used this area exclusively for the harvesting of timber.

Environmental archaeological evidence indicates that two Arctic traditions lived in this area: the Dorset culture from roughly

---

237 Heather Pringle, "Evidence of Viking Outpost Found in Canada," National Geographic News, October 19, 2012. https://www.nationalgeographic. com/news/2012/10/121019-viking-outpost-second-new-canada-science-suther-land/

238 Pringle, "Evidence of Viking Outpost

239 Wallace, "Norse Voyages."

800 BCE to 200 BCE, and the Thule culture from 1500 CE onwards.[240] Thus, during Viking exploration, there were no arctic cultures living in Markland. At this time there was, however, a First Nations culture living in the area. The Algonquin people lived in Labrador from 600 CE onwards,[241] and the children that Thorfinn captured and took back with him to Greenland were likely from this tradition.

Cape Porcupine, located slightly southward of the Hamilton Inlet, has also been suggested as the site of Markland. It has a whitesand beach and is also thought to be the location for wonder-strands, however most believe the wonder-strands are located in the Strait of Belle Isle, which runs between Newfoundland and Labrador, and the Island of Newfoundland. This places them south of Markland, but north of Vinand and L'Anse aux Meadows.

From the sagas, it is known that Hóp is located the most southerly of all the Viking settlements. It is located within Vinland, but south of Straumsfjord and Leifsbuxir. It also must be located further south than L'Anse aux Meadows, as the butternut seeds and other evidence found there were not native to the area and would have come from a more southerly location. Grapes also do not grow in L'Anse aux Meadows. The sagas indicate that there are many large islands surrounding the river at Hóp, and the river runs from a lake and into the sea. It has wild growing wheat, and lots of fish, particularly salmon.

240   William W. Fitzhugh, "Environmental Archeology and Cultural Systems in Hamilton Inlet, Labrador: A Survey of the Central Labrador Coast from 3000 B.C. to the Present," Smithsonian Contributions to Anthropology (1972). https://doi.org/10.5479/si.00810223.16.1

241   Fitzhugh, "Environmental Archeology."

Recently, Birgitta Wallace, an archaeologist with Parks Canada, stated that she believes Hóp is located in the Miramichi-Chaleur Bay area of New Brunswick.[242] It meets the criteria in several ways. This area is abundant in salmon and wild grapes, and the Indigenous group that made canoes out of hides would have also lived in this area. This bay has a river that runs into it from further inland, and further up the river there is also a lake. Many islands are dotted along the river, as well as at its mouth.

However, as the sagas illustrate, Hóp was not lived in for more than a few months at a time, though it was returned to repeatedly over the years. For this reason, Birgitta Wallace believes that it may not be a single, permanent settlement, but rather a series of short-term, temporary settlements within that general area that would have moved from year to year.[243] Certainly, as the Vikings were often under threat of being attacked by the Skraelingar in that area, it would make sense that they didn't create permanent dwellings. Because of this, she says that finding an actual site and archaeological evidence that pinpoints the location of Hóp will be extremely difficult, if it can be done at all.[244]

242   Owen Jarus, "Searching for Hóp, the Lost Canadian Viking Settlement from Lore," Genetic Literacy Project, March 13, 2018/ https://geneticliteracy-project.org/2018/03/13/searching-for-hop-the-lost-canadian-viking-settlement-from-lore/

243   Jarus, "Searching for Hóp."

244   Jarus, "Searching for Hóp."

Viking Artifact or Hoax?

Though there is archeological evidence that solidifies the presence of Vikings in North America, it seems there is a greater deal of artifacts believed to be evidence that appear to be wrongly misinterpreted as Viking, fabrications, or at the very least, that lack consensus regarding their authenticity as archeological proof. From Ontario, to Maine, to New England, various artifacts have appeared, all with suggested Viking origins.

THE VINLAND MAP

In 1965 Yale announced its possession of the Vinland Map, a 15th century depiction of a northeast section of the North American coastline. Scholars at the time had become increasingly convinced that it was not Christopher Columbus, but rather Vikings, that had first voyaged to North America, but they lacked the archeological evidence to prove it. The Vinland Map appeared to be the missing piece they had been searching for. [245] However nine years after its initial introduction to the public, a team of researchers discovered the presence of titanium dioxide in ink

245   "Historical Evidence," The Vinland Map, Brandeis University, n.d., http://vinland-map.brandeis.edu/explore/historical/index.php

fragments collected from the map. Since titanium dioxide was not a compound available until the 1900s, the team suggested the map must have been forged in the modern era. [246] Other researchers have argued that this pigment could have been produced by the overlapping of the map's different inks.[247]

Regardless of whether the Vinland Map is a forgery or not, unanswered questions about it remain. Potentially of the greatest interest is in where it came from. In 1957 an Italian book dealer named Enzo Ferrajoli first brought the map to the British Museum to be authenticated. When this authentication request was denied, Ferrajoli sold the mpa to another book dealer Laurence Witten. In 1959 Yale alumnus Paul Mellon bought the map, promising possession to Yale if they were able to authenticate it, who still own the map to this day. But where had the map been for the previous 500 years if it was a genuine 14th century artifact? Ferrajoli had claimed that he acquired it from another book dealer, but beyond that, there is no record of where the map originally came from.[248]

If the map is in fact a forgery, there is great interest in who forged it, how it was created, when, and what the motive behind its creation was. Little evidence exists to help answer any of these questions.

KENSINGTON RUNESTONE

The Kensington Runestone is perhaps the most famous

246   Kenneth M. Towe, "The Vinland Map: Still a Forgery." Accounts of Chemical Research 23, no. 3 (1990): 84-87.

247   Towe, "The Vinland Map: Still a Forgery."

248   Historical Evidence.

stone found not only in North America but perhaps out of any Runestones in Viking history. The problem: its authenticity has been debated about since nearly its discovery in 1898. Unearthed by Swedish immigrant farmer Olaf Ohman on his farm in the base of a tree the man was uprooting, the stone stands two and a half feet tall and over two feet wide, weighing 200 pounds.[249]

Inscribed on its surfaces is a description of a 1362 journey by a group of Scandinavian men from Vinland westward.[250] The stone has been on display at the Runestone Museum in Alexandria, Minnesota since 1958.[251]

First studied by Olaus J. Breda and George O. Curme, both were unanimous in their interpretation that the stone was not a 14th century artifact. Numerous analyses by Scandinavian English and German specialists corroborated the conclusion that the stone is not medieval. Two academic proponents that argue in favour of the stone's authenticity come from a linguistic professor and one Arctic ethnology professor, as well as one forensic geologist. Even with the few in favour of the stone's authenticity as a true Viking artifact, the consensus is still overwhelmingly that the stone is most likely a 19th century artifact rather than a medieval one.[252] So what has kept the interest and argument about the stone's history alive to present day?

If not a Viking artifact, then the question remains: where did the stone come from? No evidence to suggest that Ohman, the

249   Henrick Williams. "The Kensington Runestone: Fact and Fiction." The Swedish-American Historical Quarterly 63, no. 1 (2012): 3-22

250   Karri L. Springer. "The Fact and Fiction of Vikings in North America." Nebraska Anthropologist 15, (1999): 62-68.

251   Williams, "The Kensington Runestone: Fact and Fiction."

252   Williams, "The Kensington Runestone: Fact and Fiction."

one who discovered the stone, was responsible for its inscriptions nor has his account of discovering the stone ever been proven false. Alternatively, there is no evidence that either proves or disproves Viking presence in Minnesota in the fourteenth century. The only method of determining the stones age up until this point has been to study the runes and language on the stones surface—a study that is not without its own set of challenges.

While it is widely agreed by studiers of the stone that its inscriptions greater resemble more modern Swedish with potential Norweigian components than any older Scandinavian variety of language, the problem comes in needing to know both old and new versions of these languages in order to properly compare the two. One must question how many scholars that have studied the stone are in fact well versed in both. For those that are, it is likely that their knowledge of the older dialects comes from published literature, legal documents, or handbooks; jargon that would probably likely differ from a less classical version of the language used to describe the story of a voyage on the stone. Further, if the stone is in fact a forgery, the question is raised as to why the forger would not take care to copy runes from these more accessible sources?[253] So although the stone is overwhelmingly believed to be disproven as a fourteenth century artifact, this conclusion is not safeguarded from argument otherwise, or at least open to questions.

---

253   Williams, "The Kensington Runestone: Fact and Fiction."

Whether archeological fact or fiction, the mystery surrounding the Kensington Runestone has only seemed to more greatly solidify it as a cultural icon, with the authenticity debate only bringing more public interest to the stone and an overall greater public interest in the history of Vikings in North America.

But what motivates the creation of hoax artifacts, and, if not hoaxes, what drives the need for items to be interpreted as Viking artifacts? A variety of theories exist including patriotism, pride of ancestry, the necessity of some to prove their interpretation of a certain history, and if nothing else; financial gain. In the case of many of the artifacts surrounding Vikings in North America, one of the biggest motivations seems to be to provide proof that Vikings were the first to settle on North American land in a narrative that largely awards Christopher Columbus as the original explorer to discover the Americas. Although the mystery of certain artifacts surrounding the Vikings may bring more attention to this cause, they may also distort the public's perception of the actual facts surrounding the subject, such as the evidence found at L'Anse aux Meadows and perpetuate a false history.[254]

---

254   Springer, "The Fact and Fiction of Vikings in North America."

Conclusion: Rewriting History

Though medieval written records and archaeology have offered a rich insight into the vast exploits of the Norse during the Viking age and beyond, both across Europe and along the East coast of North America, it is only the tip of the iceberg; there is so much that remains unknown. The elusive settlement of Hóp has remained a mystery since L'Anse aux Meadows confirmed for the first time sixty years ago that Vikings had indeed set foot on North American land. Despite this, there is still a chance that someone may someday stumble upon evidence of it. Archaeological evidence in Markland may also be discovered in the future, and although the puzzle pieces in Helluland are beginning to fall into place, there is still so much more that might yet be discovered. The advantage of continuing to focus efforts on looking for Viking presence in the Arctic lies in the favourable climate for the preservation of archaeological material. Undoubtedly, more artifacts will be found on Baffin Island in the future.

While the archaeological story of Vikings in North America will continue to be written over the coming years, there are many details that will remain shrouded in mystery forever.

Most physical evidence of ancient peoples and places are not preserved for a millennium. The archaeological evidence that is discovered from this time period is a small exception that manages to stand the test of time.

Many parts of the saga will not be able to be proved or disproved using physical evidence. Though the reason behind the inclusion of some elements of the stories - especially those that are mythological - can be speculated about, the motive will oftentimes be unable to know with certainty. Take, for example, the description of the race of one-footed men in the Saga of Erik the Red. Thorvald (son of Erik the Red) is fatally wounded by an arrow shot by a man of the one-footed race. Historians agree that this addition to the story is wholly mythological, born out of the medieval idea that the edges of the world are home to strange, foreign, and potentially dangerous creatures.[255] At the time, multiple cultures across Europe mythologized that unipedal creatures lived in Ethiopia. As the Vikings had speculated that Vinland was an extension of Africa, it would have been plausible for them to add a uniped to the narrative to corroborate their assertion.

Many historians agree that this explanation also holds true for the civilization called Hvítramannaland, or *White Men's Land*.[256] According to the Saga of Erik the Red, the Skraelingar children captured in Markland tell the Vikings tales of this North American land. They describe the people of Hvítramannaland as having white skin and hair, dressing in white garments and

---

255   James S. Romm, The Edges of the Earth in Ancient Thought (Princeton: Princeton University Press, 1992).

256   Fridtjof Nansen, In Northern Mists: Arctic Exploration in Early Times (London: William Heinemann, 1911).

holding long poles, styling their hair with fringes, and uttering loud cries. The concept of other white - potentially European - people living in North America during and prior to its discovery by the Vikings is a fascinating one.

Hvítramannaland is not mentioned solely in the Saga of Erik the Red, but rather features in a number of Icelandic and Irish records composed during the Medieval period. Landnámabók - a detailed record of the settlement of Iceland - mentions a land called Great Ireland, located six days by boat westward of Ireland. Like most Icelandic records, the original manuscript has not survived to the present day; the earliest version of Landnámabók that survives was copied during the mid- to late-13th century.

Within this text, a man called Ari Marsson is said to have been blown off course to Great Ireland around the year 983 CE and is unable to leave. In *The Annals of Greenland* (written in the 11th century), Hvítramannaland is described as being home to a culture whose ancestors lived in Ireland. Irishmen and Icelanders happen upon the land accidentally and run into Ari. The Earl Thorfinn of Orkney corroborates this story by reporting that Ari has been sighted in Great Ireland, and the event is also referenced in the Eyrbyggja Saga.

Though most historians today believe that Hvítramannaland is entirely mythological and was likely picked up by the Norse culture through their exposure to Irish mythology,[257] others think it may have actually existed. Writer Farley Mowat suggested part of North America was populated by the priests and monks who fled Iceland and then Greenland

---

257   Nansen, In Northern Mists.

when the Vikings invaded,[258] and historian Carl Christian Rafn cited Native American legends about white men who used iron weapons and instruments.[259] Until archaeological evidence is found, it cannot be known whether Hvítramannaland was real or mythological, and this evidence is extremely unlikely to ever be found.

The possibility of making new discoveries, the questions about lands and events that will never be answered, and the already-discovered concrete evidence, are all valuable topics, as they follow a theme that has been present throughout the search for archaeological evidence of Vikings in North America: the challenging of the narrative of upper North America as empty, barren, and lifeless geographical space that was inhabited by only a few nomadic Indigenous tribes before the arrival of Christopher Columbus and John Cabot.

With even just the little evidence of Vikings in North America that we have, it is still clear that North America was not truly cut off from the rest of the world. On Baffin Island, there is clear evidence that extensive trade networks were set up between the Greenlanders and the Dorset people of the Arctic. Greenland, as a Norse colony, ultimately failed after a few centuries. Resources were scarce and winters were harsh. The Vikings would have relied on Vinland, Markland, and Helluland for valuable resources to aid in their survival, and undoubtedly took advantage of trade relationships with the Dorset people - and perhaps others - to obtain valuable items such as furs and skins. In the end, the Thule people - who are believed to have wiped out

258   Farley Mowat, The Farfarers, (Toronto: Random House, 1998).
259   North Ludlow Beamish and Carl Christian Rafn, The Discovery of America by Northmen in the Tenth Century, (London: T. and W. Boone, 1841).

the Dorset people - made their way across the Atlantic to Northern Greenland. From here, they made their way south and invaded and attacked the Norse settlements. This newfound threat was the straw that broke the camel's back, and the Norse abandoned Greenland permanently, putting an end to expeditions to Vinland and beyond.

Despite the abandonment of Greenland by the Vikings, this narrative challenges the contemporary discourse of the Arctic as an empty, bleak land. It would have been a place of great activity during the time of contact with the Vikings. If Hvítramannaland was indeed a real place, and the Minoan people did in fact travel to and from the east coast of the United States several millennia ago to mine copper, what else may have occurred? This is the tragedy of oral traditions; while they have their own unique value, they do not stand the test of time to the extent that the written tradition does. If the First Nation tribes across North America had a literary culture, imagine what those stories might tell. How many different explorers did they encounter?

What relevance does Viking presence in North America one thousand years ago have for us today? The answer to this lies in the answer to the more general question of why studying the subject of history itself matters at all. Social structures, values, beliefs, and cultural systems are built on the stories of our past; stories that we use to ground ourselves in time and space, and that we use as a justification for our current actions and identities. The wildly popular example is the reason behind why so much emphasis is placed on the remembrance of the Second World War. The atrocities committed are impossible to understand fully for those who did not live through it, yet we try. As the philosopher George Santayana once said, "those who cannot remember the past are condemned to repeat it."[260] It is for this reason we emphasize the violence perpetrated against Indigenous groups in Canada from the seventeenth century onwards. History itself is embedded in time and space, but the way we remember it is not.

In that respect, maybe it isn't history itself that matters the most, but instead the way we tell it. If we emphasize learning about and discussing the relationships between the Icelanders and Greenlanders that "discovered" Vinland, and the First Nations tribes they encountered, we contest that seemingly harmless rhyme: *In 1492, Columbus sailed the ocean blue.* Certainly, he sailed it. But was he the first? Far from it.

---

260   George Santayana, Reason in Common Sense, (New York: Charles Scribner's Sons, 1906), p. 284.

Bibliography

Bibliography

Adams Bellows, Henry. *The Poetic Edda: Volumes 1-2*. New
    Jersey: Princeton University Press, 1936.

Andrén, Jennbert, Raudvere. "Old Norse religion in religion in
    long-term perspectives." Bank of Sweden Tercentenary
    Foundation, 2006

"Anglo-Saxon Chronicle 11th Century." The British Library. n.d..
    http://www.bl.uk/learning/timeline/item126532.html

Ashworth, William. "Scientist of the Day: Haakon Shetelig." Last
    modified June 25, 2019. https://www.lindahall.org/haakon-
    shetelig/

Bailey, Richard. "Scandanavian Myth on Viking-period Stone
    Sculpture in England." Center for Medieval Studies,
    University of Sydney, 2000

Barraclough, Eleanor. "10 Myths About the Vikings." Oxford
    University Press Blog, October 2016. https://blog.oup.
    com/2016/10/ten-myths-vikings/

Beamish, North Ludlow and Carl Christian Rafn. *The Discovery
    of America by Northmen in the Tenth Century*. London: T.
    and W. Boone, 1841.

Bessel, Craig. "4 Major Misconceptions About Vikings." History Hit. Last modified October 2018. https://www.historyhit.com/major-misconceptions-about-vikings/

Bouzboune, Nasser. "The Viking Adventure in Morocco." Morocco World News Last updated March 6, 2017. https://www.moroccoworldnews.com/2017/03/210206/history-viking-adventure-morocco

Byatt, A.S. "Ragnarok: The End of the Gods." Grove Press; First American Edition, 2012

Cormack, Margaret. "Fact and Fiction in the Icelandic Sagas." *History Compass* 5, 1 (2007): 201-217. https://doi.org/10.1111/j.1478-0542.2006.00363.x.

Crichton, "Eaters of the Dead: The 13th Warrior" Vintage Books, 1997.

"Descriptio Insularum Aquilonis." Wisconsin Historical Society Digital Library and Archives, 2003

Dugmore, Keller, McGovern, "Norse Greenland Settlement: Reflections on Climate Change, Trade, and the Contrasting Fates of Human Settlements in the North Atlantic Islands." Arctic Anthropology, January 2007. https://www.researchgate.net/profile/Andrew_Dugmore2/publication/51577217_Norse_Greenland_Settlement_Reflections_on_Climate_Change_Trade_and_the_

Contrasting_Fates_of_Human_Settlements_in_the_North_
Atlantic_Islands/links/0c960514caf6d4c731000000.pdf

"Eddaic, or Eddic Poetry." Viking Archaeology. n.d.. http://viking.
archeurope.com/literature/old-norse-poetry/eddaic-poetry/

Elortza Larrea, Beñat. "Medieval Scandinavia: Power Dynamics
in the Viking Age." Medievelists.net. Last modified June,
2020. https://www.medievalists.net/2020/06/power-
dynamics-viking-age/

"Environment and Trade in the Viking Age." *Khan Academy*,
2018. https://www.khanacademy.org/humanities/
world-history/medieval-times/environment-and-trade/a/
environment-and-trade-viking-age

"Erik the Red's Saga." Where is Vinland? Great Unsolved
Mysteries in Canadian History. n.d.. https://www.
canadianmysteries.ca/sites/vinland/whereisvinland/
eriktheredsaga/indexen.html

Fitzhugh, William W. "Environmental Archeology and Cultural
Systems in Hamilton Inlet, Labrador: A Survey of the
Central Labrador Coast from 3000 B.C. to the Present."
Smithsonian Contributions to Anthropology (1972):
1–299. https://doi.org/10.5479/si.00810223.16.1

Fitzhugh, William W. "Vikings: the North Atlantic Saga."
Smithsonian Contributions to Anthropology (2000).
https://repository.si.edu/bitstream/handle/10088/22476/
anthronotes_2000_22_1_1.pdf

Gazal, Rym. "When the Arabs met the Vikings." *The National*, 2015. https://www.thenational.ae/world/when-the-arabs-met-the-vikings-new-discovery-suggests-ancient-links-1.125718

George, Jane. "Archeologist Identifies Viking Artifact near Pond Inlet." Nunatsiaq News. December 3, 1999. https://nunatsiaq.com/stories/article/archeologist_identifies_viking_artifact_near_pond_inlet/

Goodrich, Ryan. "Viking History: Facts & Myths." Live Science. August, 2018. https://www.livescience.com/32087-viking-history-facts-myths.html

Green, C.R. "A great host of captives? A note on Vikings in Morocco and Africans in early medieval Ireland and Britain," Dr. Caitlyn R. Green, Last updated September 12, 2015. https://www.caitlingreen.org/2015/09/a-great-host-of-captives.html

Gritton, Jim. "Viking Age art styles: a key to the past." 2017. https://www.researchgate.net/publication/335210353_Viking_Age_Art_Styles_Keys_to_the_Past

Groeneveld, Emma. "The Vikings in Ireland." Ancient History Encyclopedia. Last modified December 11, 2017. https://www.ancient.eu/article/1162/the-vikings-in-ireland/

Groeneveld, Emma. "Viking Art." Ancient History Encyclopedia. Last modified October 23, 2018. https://www.ancient.eu/Viking_Art/

"Historical Evidence." The Vinland Map, Brandeis University. n.d.. http://vinland-map.brandeis.edu/explore/historical/index.php

Holmes, Claire and Keith Lilley. "Viking Swansea." City Witness. N.d.. http://www.medievalswansea.ac.uk/en/context/viking-swansea/

James, Edward. "Overview: The Vikings, 800 to 1066." BBC History. Last modified March 29, 2011. http://www.bbc.co.uk/history/ancient/vikings/overview_vikings_01.shtml

Janzen, Olaf. "The Norse in the North Atlantic." *Heritage: Newfoundland and Labrador*. 1997. https://www.heritage.nf.ca/articles/exploration/norse-north-atlantic.php

Jarus, Owen. "Searching for Hóp, the Lost Canadian Viking Settlement from Lore." Genetic Literacy Project. March 13, 2018. https://geneticliteracyproject.org/2018/03/13/searching-for-hop-the-lost-canadian-viking-settlement-from-lore/

Karlsson, Gunnar. "The Natural History of Iceland." University of Minnesota Press. April 15, 2000.

Karras, Ruth Mazo. "Concubinage and Slavery in the Viking
　　Age." *Scandinavian Studies* 62, no. 2 (1990): 141-62.
　　Accessed September 15, 2020. http://www.jstor.org/
　　stable/40919117.

Kinsella, "Russia, America and the Middle East: where did the
　　Vikings visit to trade and raid?", History Extra, 2019.
　　https://www.historyextra.com/period/viking/vikings-
　　norse-raiders-where-countries-visit-impact-travell-russia-
　　greenland-america-england/https://www.historyextra.com/
　　period/viking/vikings-norse-raiders-where-countries-visit-
　　impact-travell-russia-greenland-america-england/

Kintisch, "The Lost Norse: Why did Greenland's Vikings
　　disappear?" Science Mag. Last modified November 10,
　　2016. https://www.sciencemag.org/news/2016/11/why-did-
　　greenland-s-vikings-disappear

Langer, Johnni. "The Origins of the Imaginary Viking." *Viking
　　Heritage Magazine* 4, no. 2 (2002): 7-9.

"L'Anse aux Meadows National Historic Site." United Nations
　　Educational, Scientific, and Cultural Organization
　　[UNESCO]. n.d.. https://whc.unesco.org/en/list/4/

"L'Anse aux Meadows National Historic Site: Maps and
　　Brochures." Parks Canada, Government of Canada. Last
　　modified March 30, 2017. https://www.pc.gc.ca/en/lhn-
　　nhs/nl/meadows/visit/cartes-maps

Lin, Kimberley. "Edda." Ancient History Encyclopedia. Last
      modified March 21, 2017. https://www.ancient.eu/Edda/

Little, Becky. "When Viking Kings and Queens Ruled Medieval
      Russia." History Stories. Last modified 2019. https://www.
      history.com/news/vikings-in-russia-kiev-rus-varangians-
      prince-oleg

Mark, Joshua J. ""Picts." Ancient History Encyclopedia. Last
      modified December 18, 2014. https://www.ancient.eu/
      picts/

Mark, Joshua J. "Vikings." Ancient History Encyclopedia. Last
      modified January 29, 2018. https://www.ancient.eu/
      Vikings/

McCoy, Daniel. "The Old Norse Language and how to
      Learn it." n.d.. https://norse-mythology.org/learn-
      old-norse/#:~:text=Old%20Norse%20was%20
      the%20language,of%20Norse%20mythology%20
      were%20written.&text=Speakers%20of%20Old%20
      Norse%20all,tungu%2C%20%E2%80%9CDanish%20
      tongue.%E2%80%9D

McCoy, Daniel. "The Viking Spirit: an introduction to Norse
      mythology and religion." Create Space Independent
      Publishing Platform, 2016

Menzies, Gavin. *The Lost Empire of Atlantis*. New York: William
      Morrow Paperbacks, 2012.

Mierswa, Emily. "Women Traders of the Viking Age." University of New Hampshire, 2017. https://scholars.unh.edu/cgi/viewcontent.cgi?article=1042&context=spectrum

Mowat, Farley. *The Farfarers*. Toronto: Random House, 1998.

Nansen, Fridtjof. *In Northern Mists: Arctic Exploration in Early Times*. London: William Heinemann, 1911.

"Old Norse Poetry." Viking Archaeology. n.d.. http://viking.archeurope.com/literature/old-norse-poetry/

Price, Neil. Hedenstierna-Jonson, Charlotte. Zachrisson, Torun. Kjellstrom, Anna. Stora, Jan. Krzewinska, Maja. Gunther, Torsten. Sobrado, Veronica. Jakobsson, Mattias. Gotherstrom, Anders. "Viking Warrior Women? Reassessing Birka Chamber Grave Bj.158." *Antiquity* 93, no. 367 (2019): 181-198.

Pringle, Heather. "Evidence of Viking Outpost Found in Canada." National Geographic News. October 19, 2012. https://www.nationalgeographic.com/news/2012/10/121019-viking-outpost-second-new-canada-science-sutherland/

Radner, "The Fragmentary Annals of Ireland." CELT: Corpus of Electronic Texts: a project of University College Cork, College Road, Cork, Ireland, 2004. https://celt.ucc.ie//published/G100017.html

Ray, Doug. "7 Misconceptions About the Vikings that Might Surprise You." The Franklin Institute, August, 2018. https://www.fi.edu/blog/viking-misconceptions

Richardson, Hazel. "Life of the Ancient Vikings." Crabtree Publishing Company, 2005

Roesdahl, Else. Williams, Kirsten. Margeson, Susan. "The Vikings." Penguin Books, 1998

Rogers, Sarah. "Metalworking Tool Suggests Evidence of Medieval Europeans on Baffin." Nunatsiaq News. January 9, 2015. https://nunatsiaq.com/stories/article/65674metalworking_tool_suggests_evidence_of_medieval_europeans_on_Baffin/

"Romanticism." Encyclopaedia Britannica. Last modified March 27, 2020. https://www.britannica.com/art/Romanticism

Romm, James S. *The Edges of the World in Ancient Thought.* Princeton: Princeton University Press, 1992.

Santayana, George. *Reason in Common Sense.* New York: Charles Scribner's Sons, 1906.

Sawyer, P. H. "Kings and Vikings." Taylor & Francis Group, 2003.

"Scandinavia." New World Encyclopedia. n.d.. https://www.

newworldencyclopedia.org/entry/Scandinavia

Seaver, Kirsten A. "Maps, Myths, and Men: The Story of the Vinland Map." Stanford University Press, 2004.

Sephton, John. "Translation of Eirik the Red's Saga." *Transactions of the Literary and Philosophical Society of Liverpool* 34 (1880): 183-212.

Short, William. "Games and Sports in the Viking Age," *Hurstwic*, 1999, http://www.hurstwic.org/history/articles/daily_living/text/games_and_sports.htm

Sigríður Einarsdóttir, Gréta. "A Guide to Reading the Sagas of the Icelanders." What's On. n.d.. https://www.whatson.is/guide-reading-sagas-icelanders/

Sigurd Stefansson. Manuscript Department, Royal Library, Copenhagen. Retrieved from https://www.canadianmysteries.ca/sites/vinland/othermysteries/maps/indexen.html

"Skaldic Poetry." Viking Archaeology. n.d.. http://viking.archeurope.com/literature/old-norse-poetry/skaldic-poetry/

Southon, Emma. "Boudica." *You're Dead to Me*. Hosted by Greg Jenner. BBC Radio 4, September 13, 2019.

Springer, Karri L. "The Fact and Fiction of Vikings in North America." *Nebraska Anthropologist* 15, (1999): 62-68.

"Stories, Poems, and Literature from the Viking Age." Hurstwic. n.d.. http://www.hurstwic.org/history/articles/literature/text/literature.htm

The Editors of Encyclopedia Britannica. "Sweyn II Estridsen: King of Denmark." Encyclopedia Britannica. Last modified July 3, 2007. https://www.britannica.com/biography/Sweyn-II-Estridsen

"The Vikings in Britain: A Brief History." Historical Association. Last modified January 13, 2011. https://www.history.org.uk/primary/resource/3867/the-vikings-in-britain-a-brief-history

"The Vikings in Scotland." Crann Tara. Last modified 2006. https://cranntara.scot/vikings.htm

Tikkanen, Amy. "Rus." Encyclopaedia Britannica. Last modified April 16, 2013. https://www.britannica.com/topic/Rus

Towe, M. Kenneth. "The Vinland Map:Still a Forgery." *Accounts of Chemical Research* 23, no. 3 (1990):84-87.

Tsouras, Peter. "The Fury of the Northmen." History Net. Last modified May 2014. https://www.historynet.com/the-fury-of-the-northmen-viking-assault-constantinople-860.htm

Turville-Petre, E.O.G. "Germanic religion and mythology."Encyclopaedia Britannica. Last modified March 8, 2019. https://www.britannica.com/topic/Germanic-religion-and-mythology

"Vikings." Canadian Museum of History, 2016, https://www.historymuseum.ca/vikings/

"Vikings and Settlement," Icelandic Times, 2017, https://icelandictimes.com/132318/

Wallace, Birgitta. "L'Anse aux Meadows." The Canadian Encyclopedia. Last modified March 2, 2018. https://www.thecanadianencyclopedia.ca/en/article/lanse-aux-meadows

Wallace, Birgitta. "Norse Voyages." The Canadian Encyclopedia. Last modified February 7, 2016. https://www.thecanadianencyclopedia.ca/en/article/norse-voyages

Wallace, Birgita. "Lief Eriksson." The Canadian Encyclopedia. Last modified October 12, 2018. https://www.thecanadianencyclopedia.ca/en/article/leif-ericsson

Wallace, Birgita. "Vinland." Encyclopaedia Britannica. Last modified November 9, 2016. https://www.britannica.com/place/Vinland#ref226391

"What does the word Viking mean?" Hurstwic. n.d.. http://www.hurstwic.org/history/articles/text/word_viking.htm

"What Did the Vikings Look Like?" National Museum of Denmark. n.d.. https://en.natmus.dk/historical-knowledge/denmark/prehistoric-period-until-1050-ad/the-viking-age/the-people/appearance/

"Where did they come from?" The Jorvik Viking Centre. n.d.. https://www.jorvikvikingcentre.co.uk/the-vikings/where-did-they-come-from/

"Where is Vinland?" Great Unsolved Mysteries in Canadian History. Last modified March 2007. https://www.canadianmysteries.ca/sites/vinland/othermysteries/maps/indexen.html

Williams, "Viking Religion." BBC, February 17, 2011, http://www.bbc.co.uk/history/ancient/vikings/religion_01.shtml

Williams, Henrick. "The Kensington Runestone: Facts and Fiction." *The Swedish-American Historical Quarterly* 63, no. 1 (2012): 3-22.

"Women in the Viking Age." National Museum of Denmark. n.d.. https://en.natmus.dk/historical-knowledge/denmark/prehistoric-period-until-1050-ad/the-viking-age/the-people/women/

CPSIA information can be obtained
at www.ICGtesting.com
Printed in the USA
LVHW100053290122
709443LV00012B/834